YOUR
MEDITATION
JOURNEY

YOUR
MEDITATION
JOURNEY

CHARLA DEVEREUX

*Over 30 exercises and visualizations
to guide you on the path to inner
peace and self-discovery*

Eddison Books Ltd

This edition published in Great Britain in 2019 by
Eddison Books Limited
www.eddisonbooks.com

Text copyright © Charla Devereux 2019
Illustrations copyright © Nanette Hoogslag/Debut Art 2019
Design copyright © Eddison Books Limited 2019

British Library Cataloguing-in-Publication data available on request.

ISBN 978-1-85906-438-2

1 3 5 7 9 10 8 6 4 2

Printed in Europe

Contents

· ·

· ·

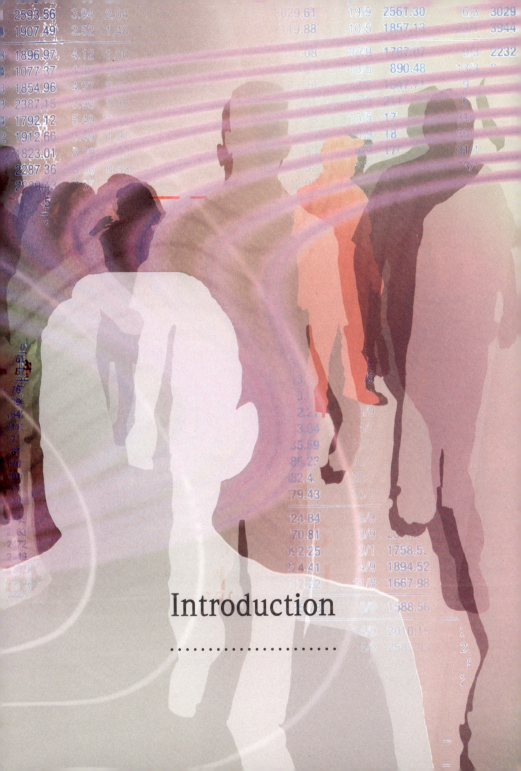

Introduction

· ·

Meditation is a system of methods aimed at attaining a mental state that is simultaneously calm, alert and focused, sometimes referred to as the 'centring' of consciousness. Regular meditation produces a controlled, balanced mind that is good not only for physical and mental well-being and effective functioning in daily life, but also for personal spiritual growth.

A Zen sage once observed that the untrained mind is like a directionless cork bobbing about on a choppy sea. That has never been truer than in today's hectic modern world where distractions pull the mind remorselessly from one thing to another. Consequently, the mental oasis provided by the practice of meditation has never been more needed. It can help you to better cope with everyday pressures, quieten the usual mental 'chatter' and add clarity of thought in decision-making.

The benefits of meditation

Although it should not be used as an alternative to mainstream, allopathic medicine, meditation is increasingly being recognized as a useful tool for helping to ease the many manifestations of stress such as high blood pressure, back pain and other muscular aches and pains, insomnia and headaches, potentially leading to overall better health. Meditation can in some circumstances also help to alleviate psychological issues such as depression and anxiety.

Because it promotes mental equilibrium and tranquillity, meditation enhances the ability to listen and understand more clearly by being really present in the moment. A state of bliss can, on occasion, be reached by a regular meditator – and even if this is attained for only a short period of time, the memory of such an experience stays forever alive in the heart and can be drawn upon, especially during those chaotic periods that life inevitably brings to everyone from time to time.

When conscientiously practised, meditation is inevitably a gateway to deep introspection, and so it can allow for greater self-knowledge and even entry to inner spiritual realms. Although approaches used in the different schools and traditions of meditation may vary, as we shall see, the ultimate aim remains the same – namely, to bring the body and mind to the highest states of sensitivity and understanding of which a person is capable of achieving.

Setting out on the journey

This book provides everything you need to enable you to effectively include the practice of meditation in your daily life. The first three chapters outline, variously, the religious, secular and scientific research backgrounds to meditation, to give a grounding in the subject and to indicate its long association with humanity. All too often in today's culture there is a tendency to seek instant gratification, with too superficial an understanding of things.

Chapter 1 provides an overview of how meditation was used in ancient religions and traditions, and you are encouraged to become familiar with this rich and important heritage. Included are examples of meditative practices in cultures that include Hinduism, Buddhism, Zen and even such shamanic-based spiritual traditions as Taoism. Meditation can also be part of the mystical side of the great global religions such as Judaism, Christianity and Islam. This longevity of meditation in human experience is your guarantee of its profound value.

Chapter 2 looks briefly at the more secular modern western approaches to meditation which tend to regard it more on a level with healing practices, such as psychotherapy, or forms of yoga.

Chapter 3 refers to a few of the growing number of scientific studies exploring both the physical and mental benefits derived from meditation, including improvement in sleep patterns, reduction in the need for medication such as tranquillizers, how meditation has been shown to have a direct effect on the patterns of electrical waves in the brain, and the possibility that different types of meditation have their own unique benefits. Modern monitoring techniques allow us to understand what takes place in the body and how it is positively affected by meditation.

Following this grounding, we learn the practical basics for setting out on your journey into meditation.

Chapter 4 includes tips on how to set up an appropriate place that you can use regularly for the purpose of meditation, information regarding some traditional postures and advice on how to prepare your body and mind for meditation – diet, clothing, time of day and sensory aids. Techniques relating to the fundamental practice of breathing meditation are also given.

The following chapters describe specific meditation techniques, bringing in rarely mentioned environmental factors in nature, such as sound and light.

Chapter 5 provides a number of guided visualization themes. Guided visualization is the best way to start reining in the mind, especially for the beginner, because being image-rich it can more effortlessly begin to train the mind on inner focusing.

Chapter 6 introduces single-point meditation. This more minimalist type of technique paradoxically requires a greater degree of mental skill. Several approaches, using both inner and external focus points, are suggested.

Chapter 7 looks at environmental factors in nature when considering outdoor meditation sessions. It describes how light and, especially, certain types of sound can be useful aids to meditation.

'Much of what may be seen as confusion in daily life can be transmuted by meditation into a more harmonious internal reality.'

The final chapter discusses the different types of silence available to the meditator.

Chapter 8 discusses both mundane silence and spiritual 'Silence'. The former is our everyday understanding of quietness, and where and when it can best be found, but the latter is the most exalted state of consciousness that can be gained in meditation if one is using it as a spiritual path. This chapter introduces koans (Zen Buddhist disrupters of logical thinking) among other techniques that help in the seeking of the Silence.

It is important to remember that although the meditative experience may not be the same for each person, the essential aim of the practice does remain the same. Much of what may be seen as confusion in daily life can be transmuted by meditation into a more harmonious internal reality which in turn leads to a more harmonious way of coping with the world. In a nutshell, the goal of meditation amounts to self-realization.

On a grand scale, we could speculate that if meditation was a normal practice within society as a whole, it would be capable of reducing much human suffering. This may sound like an ambitious claim, but it is not an idle one.

An ancient Chinese saying points out that the longest journey starts with the first step. This book can shorten the journey into meditation, so let's step out!

CHAPTER ONE

Meditation in Ancient Traditions

·····························

Health is the greatest of gifts,
Contentedness the best of riches,
Trust the best of relationships,
Nirvana is the highest happiness.

The Dhammapada
(a collection of verses reputedly
spoken by the Buddha)

In this book we will be primarily drawing on meditative traditions developed in the great religions. These are the forms of meditation most familiar to us today, but it is worth noting that meditation has been a part of human experience going back countless generations, independent of race, colour, age and gender.

Although the basic nature of meditation is fundamentally universal, it can be interpreted varyingly by different cultures. Whereas eastern religions view meditation as part of a spiritual commitment, for instance, most people today approach it in a more secularized way, treating it on a par with physical exercise, healing practices or, in some cases, psychotherapy.

Meditation through the ages

While only a brief history of meditation needs to be included here, it is useful to give at least some holistic context for understanding the nature of the practice, and the richness of its varieties.

Shamanism

One of the earliest forms of meditation was most likely developed in shamanism, in which the shaman was seen as an intermediary between the spirit world and the tribe to which he belonged. In addition to being the tribal healer, the shaman's role was to cross into the spirit world in order to gain solutions to problems affecting a particular individual or the community as a whole, or to lead the souls of dying tribal members to the spirit world. The shaman entered the spirit worlds by means of an ecstatic (out-of-body) 'soul journey' or 'spirit flight' during trance.

Neuroanthropologist Charles Laughlin has suggested that study of contemporary shamanic traditions is as close as we can come to what he calls 'the original meditation culture of the Stone Age'. In a 2018 paper, he points out that there were and still are remnants (although they are vanishing) of tribal societies that 'developed or borrowed procedures that incorporate meditation' in which initiates were trained 'in techniques of sustained attention to a set of spiritually salient symbols'. The strong mental focus and concentration that we call meditation was an essential part of instigating deeper mind states in ritual activity such as trance. He describes such meditative objects as shamanic 'mirrors', utilized in various ancient cultures ranging from American Indian tribes to Tibetan practitioners: in the Americas, shamanic mirrors could be slates that were moistened to give a darkly reflective surface, while Tibetan Tantric Buddhists used shiny metal mirrors. Other types of tribal meditation foci include star-gazing, moon-gazing, sun-gazing and crystal-gazing, collectively known by Navajo seers as deest'ii'.

There were many forms of shamanism in various tribal societies around the world, some of them still surviving, and its influence is traceable even in many of the world's great religions.

Hinduism

Meditation has its roots in the East with some of the earliest written records coming from the Hindu traditions of Vedanta, one of the schools of Hindu philosophy, in which the Vedas (texts originating in the ancient Indian subcontinent, their name meaning 'knowledge') discuss the meditative traditions of ancient India. These ancient texts provided instructions for all aspects of Hindu life. There are four Vedas and each one is divided into four parts. The fourth, or last, part of each Veda is known as the Upanishad.

The Upanishads comprise the mystical and philosophical teachings of Hinduism. It is believed that the major Upanishads were composed between 800–200 BCE. Central to them is the concept of Brahman, the ultimate reality underlying all phenomena – the source of creation. The concept of Brahman, in meditation, is used as an effective tool to expand consciousness: the main focus of Hindu meditation is to become aware of the ecstasy of the inner life, leading to the goal of attaining samadhi, meaning 'ecstatic consciousness'.

It is through yoga ('union'), a Hindu spiritual and ascetic discipline, that meditation finds its place. Yoga is made up of teachings which have come down through centuries of thought, investigation, experiment and experience. These teachings were passed on from teacher to pupil, with a definite yogic science gradually evolving in which seven systems can be distinguished. According to the teachings, the choice of system to follow is based on individual temperament; however, each system leads to the same end – experience of the Absolute, attained by advancement through various stages of development. The seven yogic systems are detailed overleaf.

○ Hatha yoga

Hatha yoga means 'force' in Sanskrit. It is concerned with the physical body and its development. The aim is to control the body and its functions. There are over eighty asanas (body postures) in hatha yoga, many of which are only taught to the highest spiritual aspirants. The purpose of the postures is to obtain the correct bodily poise that helps the mind to reach a contemplative state.

○ Laya yoga

The term 'laya' means '='. Also known as tantra yoga or kundalini yoga, it defines a type of yoga related to the stilling of the mind. According to this system, consciousness is altered by the awakening and directing of a normally dormant psychic force, known as kundalini, by transforming the base level energy into the higher levels of consciousness. Laya yoga concentrates on the chakras, which are energy points throughout the body. The seven main chakras run in a line along the spine, beginning at its base and ending with the seventh at the crown of the head. (See Appendix, page 133, for more on kundalini.)

○ Mantra yoga

This yogic system is particularly closely associated with meditation. It uses sound vibration to create an effect on the mind, the body and the emotions. A mantra is the continuous repetition of a sound vibration given by the teacher to students to affect a particular part of the body – or, more accurately, one of the chakras. Perhaps the best-known mantra is 'Om mani padme hum', or even, simply, 'Om' or 'Aum'. You will come across the use of mantras in later pages of this book.

○ Bhakta yoga

This system follows the path of the heart and can be applied to any system of yoga because no particular style or practice is specific to it. A mantra that opens the heart centre is often used. Bhakta can be found in every religion: it corresponds to the yearning for a union with the Absolute. By seeing the divine in everything, it can open the heart to love on every level.

○ *Karma yoga*

This is a discipline of selfless action by applying good deeds to everyday life. Basically, karma is the law of cause and effect. Karma yoga affects the moral attitudes in every-day life. Each person is one element of the totality and so each action affects the whole. Seeds that are planted can grow into either flowers or weeds.

○ *Jnana yoga*

This is the path of knowledge and requires enormous strength of will and intellect. It is a course of continued enquiry, seeking the answer to the constant 'Why?' Truth is continually questioned. This yoga could be called 'the union with wisdom'.

○ *Raja yoga*

'Raja' implies 'kingly' and this yoga works towards the mastery of the inner self and is reliant on independence. In a way, it is a summary of all the other systems of yoga because to practise raja one must follow hatha yoga.

Buddhism

Siddhartha Gautama, the Buddha, was born in about 560 BCE in Lumbini (now Nepal). He was the son of a chieftain and as a young man became a wandering holy man and gained the ultimate spiritual illumination while meditating under a sacred fig tree – the Bodhi Tree. He founded Buddhism, an entirely new branch of Hinduism, five centuries before the birth of Christianity. Although Buddhism had its source in the Upanishads, moral living was more important than ritual to the Buddhists and so it rejected some of the doctrines, discounting the authority of the old Vedic laws and totally discarding the doctrines of caste, theology, priesthood and the ritual of the Brahmans. Buddhism does not have gods. The essential aim – and, indeed, final goal – of Buddhism is to achieve enlightenment or nirvana, a transcendent state where there is no suffering, desire, nor sense of self, with the subject being released from the effects of karma and the cycle of death and rebirth. Buddha's teachings consisted of what are known as the Four Noble Truths (see overleaf). Part of the fourth Noble Truth is an Eightfold Noble Path which, it is thought, brings about salvation.

1. *Life is dukkha (suffering).*

2. *The cause of suffering is indulgence or desire.*

3. *By ending desire we end suffering.*

4. *The best way to end suffering is through the application of wisdom and intelligence.*

One of the stages of the Eightfold Noble Path is 'right rapture', or earnest meditation, thought and contemplation on the deep mysteries of life. The principle is to follow your own convictions and conscience, releasing yourself from formal dogma. Eventually, although not surprisingly, dogma crept into Buddhism, with the effect that Buddha became a god and nirvana a sort of heaven.

The basic Buddhist meditative technique was to simply sit quietly and to empty the mind (this being the roots of what we today call mindfulness meditation – see Chapter 2, pages 28–29). Buddhists felt that it was possible to separate attention from thought. One way was to focus on the body, and specifically what was happening to it in the present moment.

If too much attention is placed on thought, it blocks out reality: reality is the here and now, whereas thought is involved with either past or future events. Buddha taught that once the mind is empty, one will understand that nothingness is all the wisdom required in order to reach the state of ecstasy and total understanding.

As is often the case, splinter groups arose and some imposed various forms of ritual practice. These groups included Tibetan Buddhism, Taoism and Zen. The Tibetan Buddhist teacher, Sogyal Rinpoche, has in many ways summed up the essence of meditation with this statement: 'The secret is not to "think" about thoughts, but to allow them to flow through the mind, while keeping your mind free of afterthoughts.'

Tibetan Buddhism

Tibetan Buddhism incorporates elements from an earlier indigenous religion known as Bon or Bonpo, which was a kind of shamanism followed by Tibetans before the introduction of Buddhism. Tibetan Buddhists believe that the abilities of concentration and insight are basic meditation skills which are prerequisites for more advanced training. The stage of nirvana, which is understood as being liberation from bondage or freedom from the endless cycle of reincarnations, is considered to be a stage prior to bodhisattvahood, in which the disciple chooses to be reborn into the world to help others to reach salvation.

When nirvana is reached, the disciple becomes an 'arhat' (enlightened being). To reach the superior state of being a bodhisattva, the disciple must be totally motivated by love and compassion in order to become a more perfect vehicle or to be able to help others attain a state of nirvana. According to the Dalai Lama, to be a bodhisattva the disciple must 'cleanse the mind of all impurities and remove the motives and inclinations that lead to them'.

Tibetan Buddhists use single-pointedness as a meditative technique to help achieve nirvana, and state that it is a four-step process:

1. *Focus the mind on the object of meditation with prolonged concentration on it.*

2. *Let distractions come and go, while maintaining attention on the object of meditation.*

3. *Let feelings of joy and ecstasy arise, which reinforces the single-pointedness of the meditation and enables total concentration.*

4. *Total concentration comes with minimal effort.*

Some supposed secret teachings of the Tibetan Buddhists proclaim that a truth learned from another is of no value: the only truth that is of value is that which we learn for ourselves. The term 'ihag thong' is used, which means the ability to see beyond the bounds limiting the vision of the cultivated mind. One must put aside all preconceived ideas and view everything as if for the first time. This is said to be the way to knowledge.

Taoism

The word 'tao' in Chinese means 'the way'. Lao-Tzu, born in China in the sixth century BCE, is known as the founder of Taoism, a philosophical system for attaining a happy existence in harmony with Tao by advocating a life of total simplicity, naturalness and non-interference with the course of natural events.

Unlike Buddhism and Hinduism, Taoism does not believe in the transmigration of souls (movement of a soul into another body after death). Instead, Taoists consider themselves to be wanderers, in the sense that they live their life as it comes to them, without adhering to any aspect of it, nor imposing any restrictions. Taoists believe that the Tao is the principle that makes all things what they are, therefore it must not be resisted.

In common with other serious meditative traditions, early Taoism adhered to what would be considered today as strict dietary rules, with an emphasis on eating lightly. The staple diet included grain, in the form of rice or wheat, vegetables, berries, nuts, fruits, herbs, bean curd (tofu) and a very small amount of meat, poultry or fish.

There is no attempt to provide concrete rules. The Taoist approach to meditation is 'wei wu-wei' (action through inaction). No use of techniques or 'shoulds' is involved, just a settling of mental activity in order to allow deeper understanding to surface.

Lao-Tzu said, 'A good traveller has no fixed plans and is not intent on arriving.'

Zen

The term 'Zen' is derived from the Sanskrit word 'dhyana', which literally means 'meditation'. It is a form of Buddhism introduced into Japan in the twelfth century, based on the practice of an intense and concentrated type of meditation, rather than a particular philosophy or religious doctrine. In a sense, it presents a middle way between the strict practices of yoga and the understanding of the Tao. The aim of Zen is to maintain a neutral stance, or 'no mind', at all times.

Zazen (Zen meditation) uses a wide range of concentration techniques. Beginners are given breathing techniques. Other techniques involve sitting quietly with the objective being to achieve a heightened state of concentration, but without any particular object to focus on: the aspirant is aware of what is going on but does not enter into any internal commentary. The practice is simply to sit and be aware. There is an emphasis on direct intuitive experience.

A technique specific to Zen is known as the koan. Basically, the koan is a sort of puzzle that has no logical solution – meaning that the solution cannot be understood by language or thought. (Further reference to the use of the koan can be found in Chapter 8; see pages 129–130.)

When a Zen practitioner is able to achieve a point at which the distinctions between things dissolve, the state of samadhi has been reached: a mind state in which there is only a unified experience. The stage after samadhi is satori (awakenings or illumination). It is believed that with disciplined, individual effort everyone is capable of attaining this state of enlightenment. The practitioner is told to take no notice of any visions that may appear. Once satori is reached, it needs to be 'ripened' through further meditation, until it encompasses the meditator's entire life. At this point, details of everything that occurs are observed, but no appraisal is given – thus detachment is constantly maintained.

Correct posture is an important element of Zen meditation. The meditator usually sits on a pillow on the floor, with legs crossed – most often in the lotus position, in which the back is kept straight. Hands are folded in the lap with the tips of the thumbs touching. Eyes are open although lowered. It is believed that psychic powers arise naturally as the meditator reaches enlightenment. However, this is a process that normally takes many years to achieve.

An old Zen master, Hui Hai, said, 'When things happen, make no response: keep your mind from dwelling on anything whatsoever.'

Judaeo-mysticism

Roots of Jewish mysticism are found in the philosophies of the Kabbalistic teachings. Kabbalah (cabala or qabalah) means 'that which is received'. The original sense of the term was of tradition handed down by word of mouth, as distinguished from the written scriptures.

The Kabbalah is based on the Tree of Life, a diagram representing the passage of matter from its spiritual state into its final solid form, the unity believed to exist behind all things.

Kabbalists used the Tree of Life in their meditations. Their goal was to transmute the energy of the base of the tree (matter) through 'kether' (crown), into the highest manifestation of the 'ain soph' (God). The tree consists of ten sephiroth, a Hebrew term meaning holy emanations. Each branch of the tree symbolizes a development and attitude of deity as well as of man. (See Chapter 5, pages 80–84, for a guided meditation based on the Kabbalah.)

Mystical Christianity

In the fourth century, Christian monks spent much time in isolation (often in desert or mountain locations) and in what they believed to be direct communion with God. In many ways, their practices were very similar to those of the Hindu and Buddhist faiths. As an example, the use of a rosary, which is a part of Christian devotion, is a reminder of the single-pointed meditation practised by early Hindu priests. It dates back to the Egyptian anchorites.

In its complete form, the rosary consists of a chain of 150 beads divided into sets of ten beads, known as 'decades', which are separated by larger beads. The Sanskrit term 'japa-mala' ('muttering chaplet') describes the function of the rosary as a means of recording the number of prayers uttered. In the Catholic religion, the Lord's Prayer is recited on the larger beads, and the Hail Mary on the smaller beads. Each decade of beads has a special theme for meditation including such events as the Annunciation, the Crucifixion and the Resurrection of Christ. The beads are used to keep track of the progress as the devotee recites each decade.

In 1960, Thomas Merton, an American poet and religious writer, observed that what is practised as prayer in Christian churches is actually the survival of more intensive, contemplative practices. The monks living as hermits practised what would be described in other traditions as mantra meditation, involving the repetition of a very simple little prayer called the Jesus Prayer: 'Lord Jesus Christ Son of God have mercy on me, a sinner.' This is also known as the 'Kyrie eleison', which would be repeated silently and continually throughout the day. The feeling was that this sort of meditation or prayer would lead the seeker towards the highest human perfection. Such practices were widespread in both Eastern Orthodox and Roman Catholic contemplative traditions.

Indeed, prayer is commonly used in all traditional religions. However, in most of these religions it is not given in its mantric form; consequently, no shift of consciousness occurs. When praying aloud intensively, outward chatter is reduced, creating a monotonous but calming atmosphere – as is always the case when ritual words are repeated over and over.

Rituals in a church environment often involve meditational aids, such as music, the sound of bells ringing, a waft of incense, the flicker of a votive candle and the adoption of a particular posture when praying.

Wise words from the Christian sage, St Francis of Assisi: 'What you are looking for is where you're looking from.'

Sufism

Sufism is the name given to the mystical aspect of the Islamic religion. It originated in the seventh century. The word 'sufi' comes from the Arabic for 'wool' and was commonly used to describe the wool clothing worn by the early followers of this philosophy.

The main meditation technique used by the Sufis is called 'zikr', meaning 'remembrance'. Mantra is a part of this practice: repeating the name of God plays an important role in Sufi mysticism. For example, sitting in silence and continually repeating the mantra 'la illaha illa 'lla hu' (which means 'there is no God but God') produces a state of meditative consciousness. While this mantra is being recited, some Sufi sects simultaneously rotate their heads and necks in a prescribed circular motion, which helps to produce an even higher state of ecstasy.

The most popularly known Sufi meditative technique is dancing. One form of dance is a specific spinning motion (giving us the image of the 'whirling dervish'). As in yoga, the entire body is used to reach a meditative state. The use of such a method helps to release energies which are believed to be located in the spinal cord (see 'kundalini' in the Appendix). Eastern tradition believes that the release of these energies helps us to reach the meditative state.

Music is another important technique used by the Sufis to reach a higher state of consciousness. The tonal quality, in particular, helps in the meditative process. Sufis consider that certain notes activate areas in our physical being which help us to achieve higher states. For example, the high 'E' sound they use is thought to activate the so-called third eye centre in the forehead, which is supposed to affect a person's ability to achieve a different order of vision.

Rumi, the thirteenth-century Sufi mystic, stated: 'The universe is not outside of you. Look inside yourself; everything that you want, you already are.'

The story of meditation continues

We can see that meditation has been a key part in all the major ancient traditions. In the next chapter, we take a look at how meditation is perceived and has developed in modern times.

CHAPTER TWO

Modern Meditation

....

At the end of a long life dedicated to teaching mindfulness, the Buddha, who probably had his share of followers who were hoping he might make it easier for them to find their own paths, summed it up for his disciples this way: 'Be a light unto yourself.'

Jon Kabat-Zinn, *Wherever You Go, There You Are*

Today, we have access to adaptations of established, traditional meditative techniques, both religion-based and more secular. While this transplantation of ideas took off in earnest in western societies during the twentieth century, it was a process that actually began in the late nineteenth century.

East meets West

Eastern spiritual ideas were seeping into the writings of the American essayists Ralph Waldo Emerson and Henry David Thoreau, and into the poetry of Walt Whitman, but a major boost to the process occurred largely through the efforts of one controversial woman, Helena Petrovna Blavatsky.

Theosophy

The Theosophical Society was founded in 1875 in New York by Helena Blavatsky, in association with H.S. Olcott and others. The Society in general, and the person of Blavatsky in particular, represented a curious synthesis of such secular theories as Darwinism with the burgeoning cult interests of the period – particularly Spiritualism. But Theosophy also provided a royal road for Oriental philosophy to reach broader western attention, introducing concepts such as reincarnation, meditation and karma to many people.

The Society enjoyed great initial success and attracted many leading intellectuals of the day. It linked itself with a revived Hindu movement in India, and founded its headquarters at Adyar, near Madras. Blavatsky blended eastern spiritual philosophy with her own notions, the aim being to usher humanity safely along the path of evolution to a future psycho-spiritual dawn. The theme began to emerge that the Society was under the guidance of hidden masters – perfected beings living in Tibet. In 1888, Blavatsky published her main work, *The Secret Doctrine*. Various scandals broke out involving the Society, but in 1911, years after Blavatsky's death, the Society identified an Indian boy, Jiddu Krishnamurti, as the coming World Teacher of the new age. But by 1929, he had rejected the role that the Society had thrust upon him. The Society gradually declined, with people defecting, including Rudolf Steiner who founded the Anthroposophical Society. Nevertheless, the influence of the Theosophical Society was considerable and has lingered to some degree to the present day. The Society still exists.

Cultural impact of eastern traditions in the West

Western interest in Zen Buddhism was created by the Beat poets of the 1950s, such as Allen Ginsberg, Jack Kerouac, Lawrence Ferlinghetti and the San Francisco-based English writer, Alan Watts. There was a growing rejection of much of the organized concepts of religion and philosophy: more than rote-belief systems was being sought. This ultimately led to the rediscovery of the esoteric and spiritual concepts of the East – what the great English writer, Aldous Huxley, called the 'Perennial Philosophy'.

By the 1960s, a whole generation of western youth was increasingly looking for new ways to find spiritual truths.

This process was hugely aided and abetted by the so-called psychedelic revolution, which was closely linked with popular music and the arts in general. This gave the opportunity for a whole generation of people to directly experience the power of the mind through the use of mind-changing drugs. This coincided with the consequences of the invasion of Tibet by China in 1950 – the diaspora of Tibetan Buddhists, and the setting up of Western Buddhist orders. Westerners, many of them psychedelically primed, then increasingly came into contact with eastern spiritual teachers, either by journeying to India and elsewhere to sit at their feet, or as a result of such gurus visiting the West. A new traffic in spiritual ideas and practices, especially meditation, was therefore enabled, and it began to influence western society on a hitherto unprecedented scale.

Transpersonal Psychology

William James was probably the first American psychologist to include eastern ideas in his thinking. In 1893, he met Swami Vivekananda at the First World Congress of Religions, and wrote his classic, *The Varieties of Religious Experience*, which explores the psychological elements of religion.

James, along with later figures in the twentieth century such as Carl Jung, Roberto Assagioli, Abraham Maslow and Alan Watts, set the stage for establishing a new kind of psychology, known as Transpersonal Psychology, in the 1960s. This integrates into its remit the study of spiritual and 'peak experiences' beyond the ego. The Association of Transpersonal Psychology was founded in 1972, and it has gone on to develop further ever since (see Resources, page 134).

Transcendental Meditation

Transcendental Meditation, or TM, was among the first techniques that brought the practice of meditation into a twentieth–century context. Introduced to the West by Maharishi Mahesh Yogi, the system has its roots in Hindu mantra meditation and is based on the teachings of the eighth-century Indian religious philosopher, Sankaracharya. The objective of TM is to attain the union of the seeker's mind with consciousness, which is considered to be a field filling the entire cosmos.

The Maharishi first started teaching transcendental deep meditation in India. He took the practice to California in 1959 and from there his teaching spread across the US to New York and onward into Europe. The Beatles and other popular luminaries of the 1960s were influential in popularizing the TM movement. (It is said that the Beatles included in their music some of the mantric rhythms they learned in TM.) From the mid-1970s the TM movement, which has not been without its controversies, came to be increasingly structured along the lines of a multi-national corporation and has become a global phenomenon with centres in well over one hundred countries. The Maharishi died in 2008.

As with all meditation, the basic principle of TM is to reduce mental activity, allowing subtler levels of the mind to enter consciousness. The idea is to turn the attention away from the outer world of sensory experience towards the subtle, inner levels of the mind – but without actually thinking about it. TM uses mantras as meditational aids, for carrying the attention to subtler levels of the mind, to reach the source of a thought.

As its influence and resources grew, TM instigated and sponsored some interesting scientific research into mind–body interactions, particularly as exemplified in the practice of meditation. Notably, it encouraged research into the effects of meditation on the psychosomatic characteristics of stress disorders. Some TM techniques have become part of mainstream usage in both medical and corporate contexts.

Mindfulness meditation

Although mindfulness meditation has become popular in its own right, it has its roots in a number of both religious and secular traditions including Hinduism, Buddhism (especially Zen Buddhism) and yoga. Basically, mindfulness is the creation of a mental state reached by completely focusing your awareness on the present moment, which includes being conscious of your feelings, thoughts, bodily sensations and your immediate environment, without placing any judgement on them. There is no thought of past events or future possibilities, only the present moment.

In Buddhist tradition, mindfulness is carried out as a moral and philosophical system, with the mind considered to be a series of differing, transient mental states. It is used to gradually develop knowledge of oneself and the ability to see things as they are, which ultimately leads to enlightenment.

In 1971, the book *Be Here Now* by the western-born yogi and spiritual teacher Ram Dass (Richard Alpert) was considered by some to be the counterculture's bible. The book was an inspiration to the hippie movement and subsequent spiritual movements, and more than likely played a part in inspiring modern mindfulness meditation.

In 1979, Professor Jon Kabat-Zinn created the Stress Reduction Clinic and the Center for Mindfulness in Medicine, Health Care, and Society at the University of Massachusetts Medical School in the US, integrating scientific findings with his studies from a number of Buddhist teachers. He also created mindfulness-based stress reduction (MBSR), which is offered by medical centres as well as hospitals and health maintenance organizations. Kabat-Zinn feels that mindfulness can help people to cope with stress, anxiety, pain and illness. In fact, there are considered to be various health benefits associated with mindfulness meditation (see Chapter 3).

Interestingly, a paper published in 2016 reported that a relatively short, eight-week mindfulness course with a group of subjects indicated that they experienced alterations in brain activations and structure that were similar to those resulting from traditional long-term meditational practice. This was confirmed by studying the subjects' brains with functional magnetic resonance imaging (fMRI).

'In mindfulness, you focus attention on only the sensations you are experiencing in the present moment.'

One of the things that all meditation techniques have in common is being present in the moment. In mindfulness, you focus attention on only the sensations you are experiencing in the present moment. This could be anything, such as eating a snack, washing your hands, putting on your tights or socks, and so on. Daily living. The idea is to become completely focused on what you are doing, leaving no room for random thoughts.

Here are two basic mindfulness exercises to get you started. They are so easy, yet so difficult.

EXERCISE 1

Be here now

1. You are walking down a street.
2. Put away your smartphone.
3. Focus on where you are rather than where you are going. Remember that, wherever you are, you are always here.
4. Feel the breeze/wind/sun on your face.
5. Feel your feet on the hard pavement.
6. What colour are the paving slabs?
7. What are you passing? On your left? On your right?
8. What are you hearing?
9. Is it cloudy or is there a blue sky?
10. Walk on.

EXERCISE 2

The is-ness of eating an apple

1. Select an apple and slowly feel its shape, its roundness.
2. As you are rinsing it under the water tap notice the various colours of the skin.
3. Feel its waxy texture.
4. Listen to the sound made as you bite into the apple.
5. Smell the apple's fragrance.
6. Experience the flavour as it bursts into your mouth.
7. Continue to experience each bite.

This mindfulness can, of course, also be applied to eating any food – perhaps even a whole meal.

Not so easy, is it? But the more you practise mindfulness, the easier, more automatic, it becomes – as is the case with everything. Remember that if you are always *here*, you cannot get lost.

Another variation is to salvage time when travelling. For example, when travelling on a train just sit back, relax and watch the outside scenery as it passes by. No thinking, just experiencing. Got that? *No thinking* – silence that internal chatter.

Open Focus

This is another of the plethora of meditation schools that has sprung up in modern times. Psychologist Lester Fehmi, Director of the Princeton Biofeedback Centre in Princeton, New Jersey, developed Open Focus, a guided-imagery meditation which attempts to simulate a Zen-type experience of oneness with the surrounding environment by understanding the importance of how we pay attention to what is happening around us and become more open and accepting. It is closely allied with mindfulness.

Brain synchrony training, as Fehmi refers to it, is basically brain biofeedback (see Chapter 3). It shows what is happening in your brain when specific brain waves are being produced. These brain waves are the hallmark of precise forms of attention, which Fehmi identifies as Open Focus attention. Through the use of specific guided imagery, in addition to light and sound feedback, participants have reported being aware of bodily changes, for example releasing stress by relaxing their muscles.

'Our modern culture is becoming increasingly mechanistic and dehumanizing, being governed by computer algorithms rather than warm human interaction.'

All that jazz

In addition to TM, mindfulness meditation and Open Focus, there are many other schools and courses, many with catchy titles and some even claiming to be a new panacea for a variety of ailments, very often stress-related. But they are all based on meditation in one form or another.

What has brought about the rise of general awareness of meditation in today's societies (one might even say the growing need for it) is, above all, the tensions that our modern lifestyles tend to engender within us, allied to a background sense of the impoverishment of the soul. In a survey, published in 2008 by the American Center for Disease Control (CDC), of the complementary and alternative medical use of meditation, 9.4 per cent of the 23,393 US adults sampled had used meditation in the previous twelve months. For all its good points, our modern culture is becoming increasingly mechanistic and dehumanizing, being governed by computer algorithms rather than warm human interaction. It takes its toll on us. So it is not surprising that many people are seeking stress relief and, often, effective answers to their spiritual yearnings. Meditation is undoubtedly one of those effective answers.

CHAPTER THREE

Meditation,
Medicine and Science

· ·

*Look well into thyself; there is a source of strength
which will always spring up if thou wilt always look.*

Marcus Aurelius (Roman emperor and Stoic philosopher),
Meditations

An interest in meditation as a tool for relaxation as well as healing has grown in modern society since it was discovered that science is able to monitor brain waves. This has helped greatly to give meditation the credentials it needed to begin to be regarded in the West as an acceptable and useful form of practice.

It was the electroencephalograph (EEG) that initially made this possible. (The EEG is an instrument which measures the electrical activity of the brain. Small sensors are attached to the scalp, which pick up the electrical signals produced as brain cells communicate with one another.) This, and now numerous other forms of neuroimaging such as functional magnetic resonance imaging (fMRI), has allowed brain function to be studied with increasing sophistication and sensitivity, even enabling the observation of real-time changes in the brain when affected by physical or psychological stimuli.

A simpler but still useful method of measuring brain–body interactions involves testing the electrical resistance of the skin with a galvanometer. Electrodes are placed on the skin's surface and a mild electric current is conducted across it. Changes in skin resistivity can be caused by emotional or psychological stress (as in lie-detector tests): in a calm state, the skin normally resists the electric current, but in a state of stress or anxiety, skin resistance drops and enables an electric current to flow easily across it.

Interestingly, some tests have shown that skin resistance often rises during meditation. Psychologist David Orme-Johnson, University of Texas, tested whether regular meditation changes the way a person deals with stress. His hypothesis was that meditators have a greater capacity to recover from stress than non-meditators. The theory was tested on two groups, one of meditators and the other a control group of non-meditators. A loud, jarring, drilling noise was sounded intermittently, with the skin resistance of each subject being tested on each occasion. This was to see how long it would take the subjects to get used to the sound, and whether meditation helped them to tolerate it better. The answer was to be found at the point when the skin no longer reacted to the sound. For the meditators, this point was reached when the sound was heard for the eleventh time. However, the non-meditators continued to react each time the sound was repeated – forty times in all.

Further research included some of the non-meditators from previous experiments being given instructions about Transcendental Meditation (TM). Within several weeks of learning and practising TM, their galvanic skin response scores were almost as low as those of the long-term meditators.

Meditation and the brain

The human brain consists of two hemispheres. Broadly speaking, the left hemisphere deals with logic, thought, speech, planning and sequential analysis while the right hemisphere is more intuitive and can recognize individual people, read maps and enjoy art and music. (Interestingly, although it is the left side of the brain which controls speech, it is the right side of the brain that allows us to sing!) In western societies, the left hemisphere tends to be the dominant half of the brain.

Research carried out in 1975 by Dr Bernard Glueck Jr., at the Institute of Living in Hartford, Connecticut, demonstrated that people practising TM showed an increased synchrony between the left and right sides of the brain. Glueck even compared the effects of TM to taking intravenous Valium.

An area of the brain that is influenced by meditation is the amygdala (an almond-shaped mass of neurons inside each cerebral hemisphere, forming part of the limbic system), which is involved with the emotions, especially negative ones such as fear and aggression. Research by Desbordes et al. in 2012, and funded by the National

LOGICAL SIDE   INTUITIVE SIDE

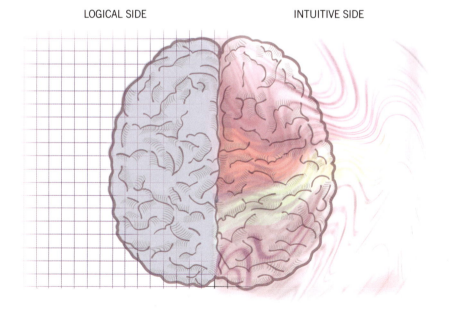

Center for Complementary and Integrative Health in the US, supported the idea that meditation can improve well-being by helping to regulate both the attention and the emotions. A reduction in activity in the amygdala correlates with experiencing less physiological reaction to stress. Furthermore, the reduction in amygdala activity seems to be a permanent pattern in those who meditate on a regular basis, indicating that the brain's response to stress is indeed altered by the practice of meditation.

In another study conducted in 2012, it was found that regular practitioners of meditation have more folds in the outer layer of the brain. It is believed that this process, known as gyrification, may increase the brain's ability to process information because the number of gyri (the irregular ridges on the surface of the brain) seems to have a close correlation to the intellectual power of the individual. Indeed, in a 2018 paper, neuroanthropologist Charles Laughlin amassed a collection of very recent papers by various researchers that back up his bald statement that 'There is now clear evidence of neuroplastic changes in brain structure as a result of the development of meditational skill.'

A rapidly growing body of research indicates that there is a close link between meditation and brain structure, and even that meditation can keep the brain younger. Normal ageing is associated with significant loss of brain tissue, but scientific measurements indicate reduced brain age in those who meditate.

Brain rhythms

The brain is electric, and brain rhythms occurring within it are characterized by their frequency. The four most common brain rhythm classifications are:

○ *Beta*
_____

Beta waves (13–30 Hz) are most common in the normal waking state when attention is focused on cognitive tasks and the outside world.

○ *Alpha*
_____

Alpha rhythms (8–12 Hz) are normally produced during wakeful relaxation when the eyes are closed, or when day-dreaming.

○ *Theta*

Theta waves (4–7 Hz) occur most often in sleep but are also dominant in deep meditation – they can often be found in the brain wave tracings of experienced meditators during their meditations. As an example, Zen monks show an ability to remain in theta for extended periods of time even though they have not actually fallen asleep.

○ *Delta*

Delta waves (0.5–4 Hz) are associated with deep sleep and dreaming – and possibly other altered mind states.

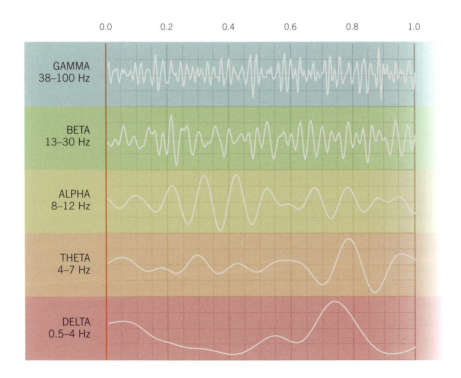

There is no doubt that meditation has a direct effect on the pattern of electrical waves in the brain. Dr Keith Wallace and his colleagues at Harvard Medical School found these effects to be quite different from the physiological changes that can be observed when simply sitting quietly, or during actual sleep. In 1971, they described meditation as a 'fourth major state of consciousness', finding that it can result in a deeper state of relaxation than sleep, as indicated by greater reductions in the metabolic rate.

There are three additional brain rhythms, which are of interest but not part of the normal experience:

○ *Lambda*

Lambda brainwave frequencies (100+ Hz) are the fastest. They are sometimes called 'ripple range', as opposed to actual 'waves'. Not much is understood about their effects but some researchers think that they may be connected to higher states of consciousness and such experiential phenomena as out-of-body experiences.

○ *Gamma*

Gamma brain waves (38–100 Hz) are associated with higher levels of insight and with peak concentration and extremely high levels of cognitive functioning. They are linked to the feeling of 'blessings' that have been reported by experienced meditators, such as monks.

○ *Epsilon*

Epsilon waves (less than 0.5 Hz) are at the other end of the frequency range, although interestingly, they are believed to produce essentially the same phenomena as lambda, which are at the top of the frequency list. Epsilon waves have reportedly been associated with yogis going into a state of suspended animation in which no heartbeat, respiration or pulse is noticeable. And yet they are fully aware and deeply relaxed.

Interestingly, an abundance of alpha waves followed by theta waves can often be found in the brain wave tracings of experienced meditators during their meditations. However, it does not follow that by bringing about certain changes in brain wave patterns we can suddenly reach nirvana. There is more to meditation than just a shift in brain wave patterning!

In the early 1970s, neurologist J.P. Banquet carried out some experiments with TM meditators which indicated that the most interesting aspect of the meditator's brain activity might not be one specific wave or pattern of waves, but the unusual evenness and rhythmic quality of whichever wave form is occurring – the tendency for all areas of the brain to harmonize and pulsate together during meditation. Specifically, the meditators were asked to push a button when they entered a new stage of meditation, with a different signal for each of five types of meditative experience. The records revealed that when four of the advanced meditators indicated that they were either in deep meditation or pure awareness, the brain wave trace showed that the alpha wave pattern shifted to a fast beta wave at the precise moment that the button was pushed. Fast beta is a waveform typical of the active, waking state. However, the beta indicated was different from the usual waking beta in that it was totally 'in phase': the recordings from different areas of the brain were synchronized. Ordinarily, waking state beta waves are uneven and unpredictable.

A clue to this synchronization effect may be gleaned from yogic rhythmic breathing. When this is practised properly, it is said that the whole system catches the vibration and becomes in harmony with the will. This is the explanation given by the yogis for their ability to increase the circulation in any part of their body, or to strengthen and stimulate any organ.

In the mid 1970s, Dr Herbert Benson, a Harvard University cardiologist, conducted an experiment comparing patients who meditated with others who did not. This was the first laboratory experiment to determine if metabolism could be lowered as a result of meditation. Additionally, it was observed that the meditating patients often needed lighter dosages of tranquillizers than the non-meditators. Also, some patients who normally had problems sleeping found that their sleeping habits improved when they meditated, allowing them to significantly reduce, or in some cases eliminate, sleep-inducing medication.

'Meditation can result in a deeper state of relaxation than sleep.'

Physiological effects of meditation

Conventional medicine is becoming increasingly aware of the extraordinary physiological benefits of meditation. Some of these many benefits include reduction of tension and the actual disappearance of many psychosomatic ailments, which can actually be stress-related symptoms, such as high blood pressure, insomnia and poor digestion. Research has shown that modern-day problems, such as anxiety, strain, over-aggressiveness, even irregular or elevated heartbeat and respiratory levels, can all be significantly decreased.

It also appears that meditation enhances muscle tone and maintains proper cortisone levels. The reason, of course, is that meditation promotes relaxation, and when the body is relaxed, there is a reduction of tension and its associated physiological symptoms. The added benefits of meditation are a simultaneous increase in general energy and overall health.

Stress is a normal reaction to physical or mental tension. However, long-term stress may be a main cause of a large range of health problems including headaches, anxiety and lack of sleep. Ongoing research is indicating that practising meditation on a regular basis can not only dramatically reduce stress but also potentially eliminate it completely. Some medical schools, as well as hospitals, are now incorporating meditational practices as a complementary method in combination with conventional approaches.

Pain control and meditation

A systematic review of the effectiveness of mindfulness-based stress reduction (see Chapter 2) in the easing of lower back pain was carried out in 2012. Three randomized controlled trials with a total of 117 patients with chronic lower back pain were analyzed. Although the evidence of the effectiveness of MBSR in improving pain intensity or disability in chronic lower back pain patients was inconclusive, there was limited evidence that MBSR can improve pain acceptance.

Another review in 2013, by K. Reiner and colleagues from the Department of Psychology, Ben Gurion University of the Negev, Israel, was carried out to investigate the specific effects of mindfulness-based intervention (MBI) on pain intensity. Sixteen studies were included in the review. The findings suggested that the intensity of pain for chronic pain patients decreased for those using MBI.

Often persisting for a month or longer, chronic pain is not always easy to identify. A study was conducted in 2016 by L. Hilton and colleagues to combine evidence on the effectiveness and safety of mindfulness meditation interventions for the treatment of chronic pain in adults. Thirty-eight randomized controlled trials were evaluated. The study concluded that although mindfulness meditation improves pain, symptoms of depression and quality of life, additional rigorous and large-scale randomized controlled trials are needed to conclusively provide estimates of the effectiveness of mindfulness meditation for chronic pain.

These are just a few of the numerous studies of the effects of meditation on pain. Research continues.

Effect of meditation on hormones

Melatonin (a neurohormone that works both as a hormone and as a neurochemical) has been shown to induce drowsiness and, when orally ingested, to alter the normal rhythms of sleep and the waking state. Melatonin is produced by the pineal gland, which is thought to secrete it during theta and delta brain wave activity. The pineal gland is a small, cone-shaped organ, located in the centre of the brain near the hypothalamus and the pituitary gland. It was thought by modern science to have no function and even now its full function is not completely understood. However, eastern mystics believed that the pineal gland, also known as 'the third eye' or 'seat of the soul', is directly involved with meditation and clairvoyance.

Two studies in the late 1990s, one conducted at the University of Massachusetts Medical Center and the other being a Saybrook University doctoral study conducted at the University of Western Ontario Research Park, suggested that there is a link between meditative practice and an increase in the supply of melatonin. This was established by measuring the major melatonin metabolite in urine. The study in Massachusetts recorded the difference between the levels of melatonin in eight experienced meditators versus a control group of the same number of non-meditators. A higher level of melatonin was found in the meditators. Ranjie Singh, who conducted the Saybrook study, was also interested to see if a combination of mantra, visualization and special breathing techniques, known to induce deep meditation, could stimulate the pineal gland, as measured by the level of melatonin in the urine. The study showed an increase in urinary levels of melatonin after these practices.

Melatonin is known to be a primary regulator of the immune system, responsible for preventing cancer cell growth. As a result of these trials linking meditation to the increased production of melatonin, studies have been conducted looking at the effects of meditation on women in the early stages of breast cancer. For example, in 2016, researchers at Michigan State University published their findings that melatonin appears to suppress the growth of breast cancer tumours. It was felt that the results of their study give scientists a key foundation on which to build further research, including the effects of meditation on men in the early stages of prostate cancer.

(Please note that the research is only studying levels of naturally produced melatonin.)

Effect of mantra meditation on moods

The eastern teachers were able to sense intuitively the physical and psychological needs of their disciples. They would then choose a sound vibration, or mantra, that according to their belief would benefit the spiritual and physical well-being of the disciple. After a period of time, which could be short or long depending on the disciple's innate ability, the mantra would produce an almost alchemical change in the individual.

In 1976, an experiment was carried out at Princeton University, by researchers Douglas Moltz and Patricia Carrington, to formally investigate the effects of word sounds on mood. They chose, at random, single-syllable sounds which had no particular meaning in the English language. Fifteen such 'nonsense syllables' were selected, five of which seemed to be very soothing, another five of which were rather jarring and a further five of which conveyed a neutral effect. The list of sounds was given to one hundred subjects, who were asked to mentally repeat each sound and rate it on a seven-point graded scale which ranged from 'extremely soothing' to 'extremely jarring'. As there was a high percentage of agreement, it was easy to select three sounds, one from each group.

The three selected sounds were then presented to a group of thirty students, none of whom had ever meditated before. They were asked to repeat each of the sounds silently for a period of five minutes. At the end of each five-minute period, they were asked to describe their mood while repeating the particular sound, by selecting one or more adjectives from a checklist. (It should be noted that before being given the first sound, the students were asked to mark the adjectives that best described their mood just before the start of the experiment.) The object was to see if different word sounds had different effects on mood, thereby testing the claim of the meditative traditions that particular mantra have particular effects.

The three sounds chosen were 'lōm', 'noi' and 'grik'. The results showed that the repetition of the sound 'lōm' caused a significant decrease in anger and hostility, while 'grik' had the opposite effect, causing an angry and irritable mood to increase significantly. (However, it was discovered that repeating the word 'grik' also caused a reduction in depression and dejection. What is of interest here is that, according to a well-known clinical observation, when a depressed person feels anger at something or someone outside him or herself, the depression often disappears.) There were other findings as well. Both the sounds 'lōm' and 'noi' had positive effects on feel-ings of fatigue. And of the three sounds, 'noi' was the only one which had the effect of reducing tension and anxiety. In short, this preliminary study demonstrated what the earlier cultures who practised mantra already knew – that sound can affect human mood.

When various traditional mantra sounds are examined closely, most of them end in a resonant nasal sound, such as 'n', 'm' or 'ng'. The best-known mantra, 'Om', is a case in point. These sounds seem to reverberate internally. Of course, we must take into account any mental associations we may have for a particular word. These associations are usually individual, while certain sounds carry a universal meaning.

Nature's way

A growing body of evidence is indicating that meditation has a positive effect on a wide variety of health issues, in addition to what has already been touched upon here, including memory loss and helping people to stop smoking. The debate on the effects of meditation for all kinds of conditions will continue, because there is no doubt that for western society it is more than just a passing phase. This has never been timelier, because people suffering the dysfunctions that result from physical stress and anxieties, engendered by the lifestyles to which we are so prone today, are too often prescribed 'happy pills' – a chemical fix for the problem. Not only does this tend to mask real problems rather than trying to solve them, it can also lead to drug dependency and further complications, as has been exemplified by the recent controversies such as the opioid crisis in the US. Meditation offers nature's way of at least partially dealing with such difficulties.

CHAPTER FOUR

The Basics of Practical Meditation

. . . .

*The gift of learning to meditate is the greatest gift
you can give yourself in this life. For it is only through
meditation that you can undertake the journey to
discover your true nature, and to find the stability
and confidence you will need to live, and die, well.*

Sogyal Rinpoche, *The Tibetan Book of Living and Dying*

The reason for deciding to meditate can be as straightforward as simply wanting to learn how to relax, to reduce the stress of daily life and gain the health benefits that come from that. Or, you may find it a useful tool to assist in a personal spiritual quest. Whatever the reason, some basic preparation is helpful, as in any endeavour in life. This chapter offers advice for helping you to prepare a dedicated place in your home for meditation, as well as suggestions about how to physically prepare yourself, with an emphasis on posture and breathing.

First, and simply, relax and enjoy the experience of meditating without placing any expectations on yourself. It is not a test, nor is there a limited time period for achieving results. By making meditation a regular part of your lifestyle, the benefits will become obvious.

The meditation space

Deciding where to meditate is a significant first step. Of importance is finding a quiet place where you will not easily be disturbed, either by outside noise or other people in your immediate environment. It is, of course, best to make those around you aware that for a specified period of time you do not want to be disturbed. If there is a phone near your chosen place, be sure to turn it off, including any answering machine, as a voice message coming through would obviously be distracting. Turn off your mobile phone too.

Some people are fortunate in being able to devote an entire room to quiet pursuits such as reading or meditating. Failing that, a dedicated corner with some sort of centring device, such as a plant or vase of flowers, a small sculpture or picture, or some valued object, will work. Whatever your situation, the key thing is to use the same place for your meditation sessions on a regular basis. By doing so, you will be creating an 'atmosphere' that will reinforce the purpose of the space, building up a quality that is tangibly different from every other part of your home. It will act as a signal for meditation.

A softly lit space adds to the type of ambience that aids in creating a peaceful state of mind amenable to meditation. While candlelight may be a good option for an otherwise dark room, depending on circumstance this might not be practical.

A low-power or coloured light bulb is another possible option. Some people prefer no lighting in the room at all, with just the hint of light coming from an adjacent room. If your chosen time for meditating is during the day, be sure that the blinds or curtains are drawn so as to keep out glaring sunlight.

At times, you may want to meditate out of doors, so be sure to select a location where you are not likely to be disturbed. Some other factors about choosing outdoor meditation places are discussed in Chapter 7.

Incense

There is no more effective a way to make your meditation space 'special', and suitable for its purpose, than the use of incense. It is interesting that, of our five senses, the sense of smell has the most direct connection to the brain: the effect of smell is immediate, because the olfactory bulb is directly connected to the brain. The average person is able to recognize as many as ten thousand different fragrances. A smell, therefore, can actually trigger an emotion before we are consciously aware of it. A familiar smell can be linked instantaneously to a past event – the fact that an odour can provoke memory is one of the aspects of the sense of smell that relates to meditation.

You can work with fragrance in your meditation space in various ways. One is to use scented candles. Another is the use of incense cones or joss sticks, although some people may find their strong scent too overpowering. A third option is to use a fragrance produced by vaporizing essential oils. If you do not have a diffuser (specially designed to disperse the fragrance and readily available in shops and online), you can place several drops of the oil on a ball of cotton wool and hold this in your cupped hands. Simply inhale the fragrance as you shut your eyes.

'The sense of smell has the most direct connection to the brain; a smell can trigger an emotion before we are consciously aware of it.'

The oils you choose to work with will depend on the atmosphere you desire to create, or the particular situation you want to work on. The scent of roses, for example, is extremely uplifting, and burning rose essential oil in a diffuser is an effective anti-depressant. These qualities make rose oil an excellent scent for creating a warm and protective atmosphere when meditating. Melissa, mandarin and rosemary fragrances are also noted for their ability to produce an uplifting effect.

The relaxing, warming and balancing qualities of geranium make it the perfect fragrance to use when wanting to create a balanced atmosphere. The inhalation of geranium also has a calming effect on the body and mind.

But it is frankincense that has been recognized as having a particularly powerful influence on the mind, and it has been used in rituals and ceremonies for thousands of years. It was such a precious commodity in ancient times that wars were fought over it. The inhalation of frankincense is said to heighten spiritual awareness and the deepening of religious or magical experiences. It has a calming effect and is one of the most popular oils for meditation as it helps to slow the rate of breathing. In short, frankincense is arguably the ideal fragrance to use generally when meditating.

EXERCISE 3

Focusing on fragrance

The sense of smell can provide a meditation exercise in itself, quite apart from giving your meditation space a distinctive identity.

1. Adopt your favoured posture (see suggestions on pages 55–59), close your eyes and focus exclusively on the fragrance you have chosen, and allow the scent to take you on a journey of discovery. Welcome it in. If it conjures memories or associations for you, try to observe them dispassionately, but the nature of those memories or associations will tell you much about the mental cargo, positive or negative, you are carrying. You may be surprised to find that you remember things associated with the fragrance which you had not thought about for a long time – which until now were buried deep within your own memory. Let the fragrance tell you about yourself.

2. When you feel ready, probably after about ten or fifteen minutes, gently open your eyes. Quench the fragrance but be aware that when you use it again for a meditation session it can act as a shortcut for future inner exploration.

This type of meditation may also be useful to help you understand why you feel a particular way about a fragrance. For example, a friend had a strong dislike of frankincense, but by burning some frankincense oil in a burner during a meditation, the friend was able to remember what made him dislike it: when he was a child, he did not like to go to church because it meant that he had to sit quietly for what seemed like an endless period of time. Understandably, for a young child who would rather be outside running and playing with his friends, sitting in church for long periods was boring and unpleasant. Part of the church ceremony included the burning of frankincense. The fragrance was associated with this childhood memory, so he still found the odour unpleasant. Once this association was understood, it no longer bothered him.

Preparing the body

Of utmost importance is that you are comfortable before you start your meditation session. If the room temperature is right, you will probably not notice it at all. But if you do, and you cannot easily adjust the temperature to your liking, then it might require a change of clothing. It is also important to know that body temperature often falls slightly during meditation – nothing to worry about, as it is a normal reaction, but good to keep in mind when deciding what to wear.

Whatever your choice of apparel, it is best for it to be loose-fitting so that any movement is completely unrestricted (this is especially the case if you are planning to sit on the floor in a yoga posture). It is also best to avoid wearing shoes. Either bare feet or soft-fitting socks are suggested.

Nutrition

As your physiological state can play a part in the quality of your meditational experience, it is helpful if you do not feel either hungry or full. Best to wait for at least thirty minutes after eating, and perhaps longer, depending on the size of the meal. Some people consider that a controlled fast can be conducive to the focusing of attention – indeed, yogis very often fast prior to meditation. Some people make a point of meditating in the morning before having breakfast.

Because what you eat can have an effect on your mental function, it is important to avoid foods that have a negative influence. Of course, a sensible diet is not only advantageous to meditation, but essential for overall well-being. As a general guideline, emphasis on fresh fruits, vegetables and carbohydrates (not the sugary kind) would be best, if eating prior to meditation, in addition to avoiding stimulants such as coffee, tea and soft drinks containing caffeine. For a drink, just a glass of water would be best. It is well-attested folklore that what happens in the stomach can have a direct effect on what happens in the head! A well-functioning digestive system provides the optimum bodily condition for meditation.

Time considerations

While some people may prefer to meditate in the early morning and others in the early evening, the best time for meditating is the time that suits you so that it can become part of your daily routine as much as possible. Inevitably, for most people, the time available is determined by other events such as work schedules and family commitments, so in many cases the time to meditate may already be chosen for you!

If you are able to set aside time in the evening, it can be helpful in getting over any stresses from the day. Meditation in the evening can also be very helpful in obtaining a good night's sleep.

Alternatively, if time is available, you may prefer to start your day with a meditation, to set you up for what the day may have in store for you. Indeed, if finding time is not an issue, you may even be able to meditate twice a day.

Whatever your situation, meditating at the same time in your daily routine is the ideal – same place, same time. This will help you to adapt more readily to the meditative state so that entering it will get easier, because you are in effect programming yourself to meditate at a specific time each day. It is best not to have any pressing commitment directly after your meditation session, so you are not pressured into setting a time limit. However, do not feel guilty if sometimes you simply cannot fit in your time to meditate on a particular day.

While there are no hard and fast rules about the amount of time spent meditating, a guideline is anywhere from twenty minutes to one hour, depending on the type of meditation you are doing. It can often take up to fifteen minutes just to settle the mind before even starting to enter the meditative state. (Of course, people who are very experienced in deep spiritual meditation can remain in that state for an indeterminate period of time.)

If time is not a consideration it is wise to allocate up to twenty minutes at the end of your meditation session to allow you to quietly emerge from the meditative state.

This provides your body and mind with a smooth transition period before returning to 'normal' consciousness, as well as enabling you to enjoy the peaceful atmosphere that the meditation is likely to have created.

If it is necessary to set a specific time limit for your meditation, then think carefully about how you can signal that time is up. As the use of a timer can be rather jolting, you may consider burying it under a pillow or two to muffle the sound. Another option would be to set a timer on a CD clock so you can end the session with the onset of carefully chosen calm music.

There is, of course, no pressure for you to have to meditate in specific allotments of time: very often those new to meditation find that even ten minutes' meditation is difficult to achieve. Don't be discouraged. The suggestions here are only guidelines. You will need to determine what is most suitable for you.

Body rhythms

Similar to the ocean cycle of tides, the body has its own daily rhythm known as the circadian rhythm, although it is more often referred to as the 'body clock'. Basically, the circadian rhythm is a daily rhythmic activity cycle based on twenty-four-hour intervals. This cycle is affected by environmental signals, such as sunlight and temperature, and it lets our bodies know when it is time to sleep, wake, eat, and so on. Many of these rhythms are obvious, such as when you start to feel hungry or when your energy is at a low point, but other changes that happen are less noticeable, such as the small shifts in body temperature that occur in the course of the day, often from a low point in the morning to a high point in the afternoon. (This is a normal occurrence for most people who sleep at night and are active during the day.) Most bodily functions, such as blood sugar levels and kidney functions, are subject to daily rhythms. These types of cyclical changes in our adrenal hormone level can also affect the way we react to stress. Like other functions of the body, our hormone level follows its own pattern of high points and low points. These can sometimes be linked to external cycles such as day and night.

Through meditation, you can tune into these internal body rhythms, becoming more conscious of them. Being able to meditate more than once a day, even if not consistently, will give you the opportunity to see how you may be affected by your meditation, depending on the time of day. For example, you may find that morning meditation can act like a tonic, energizing you for the day ahead, while an evening meditation may have just the opposite effect, producing an almost lethargic reaction.

Posture

While there is flexibility regarding the position preferred for meditation, there are some basics that really should be employed concerning posture. Comfort is an important factor, so if sitting on the floor is not for you, then sitting on a stool, chair or couch is perfectly acceptable. What is important, though, is that you maintain a straight position with your neck, head and back in vertical alignment (imagine that there is a string held taut from the top of your head, pulling upwards).

If using a chair, it is best to use one with a straight back, positioning yourself near the front edge of the seat and keeping your back as straight as possible, avoiding any tendency to lean against the back of the chair. However, if using a well-worn sofa or a soft armchair, be sure to prop yourself up with some firm pillows or cushions. In all seated positions, if not adopting a yoga posture, keep both feet flat on the floor. Your hands should rest comfortably so as not to be distracting. Place them close to your knees or in your lap, palms up or palms down. You may prefer to keep them apart, or hold one hand cupped in the other.

You may favour sitting on the floor but, unless you are used to it, you could find yourself fidgeting and focusing on the ache in your back instead of your meditation! Using a cushion can help, but be sure that the back of the cushion is slightly higher than the front, thus forcing the pelvis slightly forward.

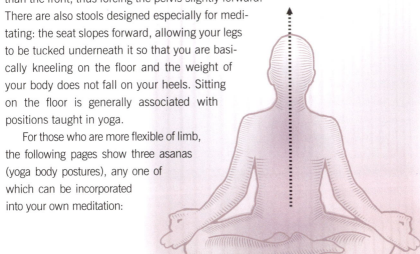

There are also stools designed especially for meditating: the seat slopes forward, allowing your legs to be tucked underneath it so that you are basically kneeling on the floor and the weight of your body does not fall on your heels. Sitting on the floor is generally associated with positions taught in yoga.

For those who are more flexible of limb, the following pages show three asanas (yoga body postures), any one of which can be incorporated into your own meditation:

○ *Sukhasana*

This is the easiest of all the asana postures, consisting of sitting cross-legged on the floor. First, sit on the edge of a small, low cushion. Once you are comfortable, stretch your legs straight out in front of you. Slowly bend the left leg towards your body and tuck the left foot under the right thigh. Now do the same with the right leg, tucking it under the left thigh.

This posture allows the body to be held erect. Your hands should be spread loosely, palms facing up and resting gently on or close to the knees, thumb and forefingers curved into a circle with the tips joining (this finger position is optional). Or you may prefer to rest your hands with the palms facing down on your knees.

Stop when you start to feel any discomfort: you may well find that you need some time to build up to being able to maintain the posture for longer periods.

○ *Padmasana*

Of all the yoga postures, this is probably the most familiar to the West. It is called the lotus pose because the position of the feet resembles lotus petals. Although this pose is often found to be difficult, if not physically impossible, for some people to attain, it is offered here for those who wish, and are able, to use it as part of their meditation practice.

The lotus pose is more easily attained by people with supple limbs; it may take longer for those who have taken up yoga postures at a later age.

Sit on a small cushion on the floor, close to the edge of the cushion (this gives support to your spine). Extend your legs forward. Take hold of your left foot with both hands and place it on your right thigh, with the sole of the foot turned upwards. Now take your right foot and bring it up over the left leg, so that it can be similarly placed on the left thigh. (At first, you may find it difficult to get the right leg over the left leg.) After you have used this pose for a while, you may well discover a new supple condition of limbs, body and mind.

○ *Siddhasana*

It has been suggested that this pose was often used by mystics, who were thought to be perfect, hence its name: the pose of perfection.

Start by sitting on the floor, sitting close to the edge of a small cushion. Extend both legs straight out in front of you. Take your left foot in your right hand and gently draw it towards your body so that the left heel can be placed directly beneath you, with the sole of the left foot touching the right thigh. The left leg must be completely doubled up in order to achieve this posture. Then bring your right leg over, so that it is also bent double, with your right foot resting above the left ankle, and your toes resting gently between the calf and thigh of your left leg.

The body will be kept erect. Choose any of the hand positions described in the sukhasana. Make sure the one you choose is comfortable so that you are not distracted. This pose may well require considerable practice, but do not be discouraged: it can be attained.

Whether you decide to sit on a seat or on the floor, remember to keep your spine as erect as possible in order to achieve a good balance of relaxation and alertness. One can meditate while walking, though this can lead to distractions, or even lying down, but the latter is to be discouraged unless for medical reasons, as it can all too easily encourage sleepiness and also prevents the vertical erectness of the spine.

If you find at any time during your meditation that you begin to feel uncomfortable, do not hesitate to shift and change position slightly, otherwise your focus will be more on the discomfort than the meditation. Trying to remain perfectly still while feeling nagging discomfort in your back or neck will only make you lose concentration and will detract from the meditative process. Master yogis have learned to overcome all physical discomfort, but we can allow ourselves more flexibility!

Breathing

Once you have arranged your meditation space and made yourself comfortable, the next step is to completely relax your body. The natural – and, as it happens, most powerful – way to do this is through the breath. The yogic tradition of controlled breathing, or pranayama, is considered to be the foundation of the practice of yoga. This is also true for meditation. Regulating the breathing pattern is an essential part of calming the mind. When breath is controlled, not only can it help to attain a state of altered consciousness, it can also bring about a whole physical regenerative process.

There are three common respiratory processes. Starting with the shallowest and progressing to the deepest, they are:

○ *Breathing from the chest*

Chest, or shallow, breathing inhibits the range of motion of the diaphragm, which in turn limits the amount of oxygen reaching the lowest portion of the lungs, sometimes resulting in a feeling of anxiety due to the shortness of breath. Rapid shallow breathing can even cause loss of consciousness.

○ *Breathing from the ribs*

In rib breathing the diaphragm is pressed upwards and the abdomen is drawn in. Although this gets more air into the lungs than chest breathing, it does not give the lungs the chance to obtain full capacity.

○ *Abdominal breathing*

This is the ideal. Abdominal, or deep, breathing is primarily done through an action of the diaphragm (the dome-shaped muscle separating the chest and abdominal cavities). As you breathe in, the diaphragm pulls your lungs downward. The abdomen extends as the diaphragm lowers, allowing more capacity for the lungs to expand as they fill with air. With your outbreath, the diaphragm lifts back against your lungs, which helps to expel carbon dioxide.

Deep abdominal breathing allows a full exchange of oxygen – exchanging incoming oxygen for outgoing toxins. In addition to a controlled heartbeat, this deep abdominal breathing can also lower or stabilize blood pressure.

IN   OUT

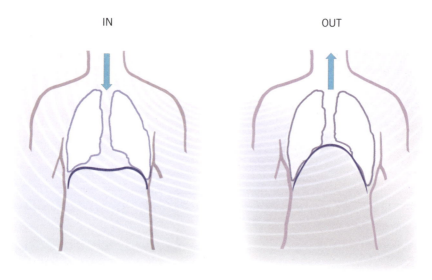

The complete yogic breath (see below) incorporates all three breathing processes and is designed to exercise all parts of the respiratory tract and lungs. The cleansing breath (see overleaf) is also a valuable yoga breathing technique, good to use at the end of a meditation.

It is important to always breathe in through the nose, because nasal breathing filters out impurities in the air, something that inhalation of breath through the mouth cannot do. In addition to providing a protective filter, inhaling through the nose also warms the air to a temperature suitable for the body. Breathing in cold air through the mouth can result in inflammation of the respiratory organs.

EXERCISE 4

Yoga complete breath

1. Sit erect and breathe in through the nostrils, first filling the lower part of the lungs, then the middle and finally the top. This should be done in one slow and steady breath.
2. Hold the breath for a few seconds.
3. Exhale slowly through the nostrils, keeping the chest in a firm position while slightly drawing in the abdomen.
4. Lift the chest upwards slowly as the air leaves the lungs.
5. Once the air has been exhaled, both chest and abdomen can be relaxed.

EXERCISE 5

The cleansing breath

1. Deeply inhale and hold the air for a few seconds.
2. Pucker the lips and vigorously exhale some of the air through the mouth.
3. Pause, holding the remaining breath for a few seconds before exhaling a little more of the air.
4. Continue alternating between exhaling some breath and pausing until all of the air has been exhaled.

Some additional basic yoga wisdom

In yogic tradition, it is believed that when we breathe, in addition to inhaling oxygen, hydrogen and nitrogen, we also breathe in prana (a Sanskrit word meaning 'life force'). Yogis believe that prana is necessary for every thought and motion. It is found in all living things, and is considered to be the active principle or vitality of life itself. This is one of the reasons why yogis feel that proper breathing is so important because it provides a constant supply of prana.

Regardless of whether or not this is literally true, there is little doubt that in daily life most people are taking in less oxygen than their bodies are capable of processing. Ideally, deep breathing should be part of normal breathing as it floods the body with extra energy and also helps to calm the mind, something equally beneficial in meditation as well as daily life. (According to folk wisdom, when you feel frustrated or irritated all you need to do is to take in several slow, deep breaths, and you will feel almost instant relief.)

Controlling the breath

The importance of keeping an even rhythm when inhaling and exhaling is emphasized in all the breathing techniques described below.

One very basic breathing technique, which can be used any time you feel the slightest bit of stress, is to inhale slowly and fully as you visualize the air (perhaps in the form of light) entering your nostrils. Exhalation, through the nostrils, should be a smooth and steady release of the breath, the whole process becoming a gentle, wave-like rhythm, like the ebb and flow of the sea. Just taking a few minutes for yourself to breathe in this way will make a big difference to how you handle any given situation.

EXERCISE 6

Rhythmic breathing technique

1. Sit motionless in an erect position. Breathe in slowly and steadily through the nostrils, and be aware of the downward motion of your diaphragm and the extension of your abdomen.
2. Continue to inhale, feeling the air filling the middle and upper lungs. Hold the breath for a short period and then slowly exhale, through either the nose or mouth, gently forcing out as much air as possible.
3. As you take your second breath, slowly count to yourself until your lungs are full.
4. Next, hold your breath, counting for half the time it took to inhale, then begin to exhale, counting up to the same number as when you inhaled.
5. Finally, hold your breath for half the count before beginning the process again, using the same inhalation count as before.

There is no correct number of counts for the above exercise; it is simply about finding what feels comfortable to you. What is important is that the same number is used for the exhalation as for the inhalation, with half that number when holding the breath. So, for example, if you slowly count to six on the inhalation, then you need to count to three when holding your breath and then six again for the exhalation and three for holding the breath before starting again. While this technique is good to use at the start of your meditation, it can also be used as a meditation itself if you focus full attention on the breathing rhythm.

Once you thoroughly have the rhythm, you can stop the mental counting, bearing in mind that although this may sound easy, you may discover how difficult it is to concentrate on even a basic bodily function such as breathing. Almost before you are aware of it, your attention can begin to wander. But do not be discouraged, because with practice this kind of conscious breathing will soon bring calm and order to the normally chaotic mental processes. What is important to keep in mind is that the way you breathe can have a direct bearing on the quality of your meditation.

A slight variation on the previous technique, and one often used by yogis, is to synchronize your rhythmic breathing with your heartbeat (see Exercise 7, opposite). You may be surprised to learn that one nostril is generally dominant over the other when you breathe, and that dominance changes approximately every few hours.

It has long been understood by neurophysiologists that the right hemisphere of the brain – which in general terms causes a person to be passive and introverted – controls the left side of the body, while the left hemisphere of the brain – which performs tasks concerned with logic and analytical thought – controls the right side of the body. Similarly, according to yogic belief, the left nostril affects the right hemisphere of the brain. It is for this reason that in the method of swar yoga, which means unification through the breath, the left nostril is the preferred dominant nostril during the meditative process. This is because it is believed that when the right nostril dominates, the individual is likely to be easily distracted.

Fortunately, you do not have to necessarily wait for the preferred situation because nostril dominance can be easily achieved by lying on the right side of the body for a few minutes before meditation and letting gravity do the work by draining the sinuses.

(For more in-depth information about the importance of breathing properly, I recommend Richard Brennan's insightful book *How to Breathe*.)

EXERCISE 7

Pulse count

1. After you have made yourself comfortable, place your fingers on your pulse and count the beats as you breathe until the rhythm becomes firmly fixed in your mind (on average, it usually takes about six counts or pulse units to fully inhale, but this is only an average so count up to whatever number is comfortable for you).

2. When you have fully inhaled, hold your breath for a few counts before gently exhaling, using the same number of counts as you did when inhaling. Continue this practice until your mind is quiet and you are totally at ease.

You may find it easiest to follow the yogic rule for rhythmic breathing, as described in the previous exercise, where the number count for inhalation and exhalation should be the same, while the count for retention and between breaths should be half that number.

Muscle Tension Release

Muscular tension is very often a consequence of stress. A simple muscle relaxation exercise can be used, or combined with your chosen deep breathing technique, for additional stress relief. The idea is to purposefully tense and then relax each muscle group in the body, one group at a time. However, if you have a history of injury that may be affected by this, such as a back problem, it is recommended to first consult your doctor.

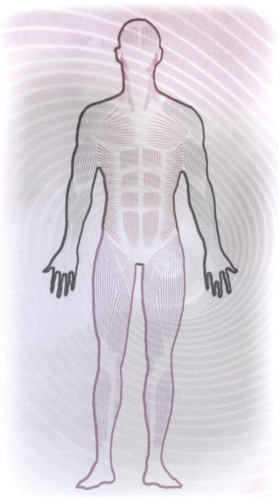

EXERCISE 8

Relaxing muscles one group at a time

1. After getting comfortable and using the rhythmic breathing technique described on page 63, turn your attention to your feet. Slowly tense the muscles in your feet, squeezing your toes together as tightly as possible, count to five and then release the muscles. Give yourself a few seconds to feel the difference in how your feet feel.

2. Repeat the exercise, moving up your body: tense and relax your calves, thighs, hips and buttocks, arms, hands, stomach, chest, back, shoulders, neck and finally, your face.

3. There are many small muscles in the face, so relax the lips and tongue, perhaps letting the jaw hang slightly loose.

4. Then relax the many tiny muscles round the eyes until the eyelids feel heavy.

Happy ending

When you have completed your meditation, regardless of what techniques you use, it is important to allow yourself time to slowly return to your normal waking consciousness so that the tranquillity you experienced during your meditation can seamlessly flow into your waking state. It can also be useful to incorporate a few stretching exercises before resuming your normal routine.

CHAPTER FIVE

Guided Visualization: Starting the Inner Journey

....

I will arise and go now, for always night and day
I hear lake water lapping with low sounds by the shore;
While I stand on the roadway, or on the pavements grey,
I hear it in the deep heart's core

W.B. Yeats, *'The Lake Isle of Innisfree'*

Meditation, which is the focused inward turning of consciousness, requires patience and practice, but the more you do it the easier it becomes. For the beginner, guided visualization is the best way to start reining in the mind because, being image-rich with a narrative thread, it can more effectively begin to engage the mind on inner focusing. Again, practice is the key.

There are claims that guided visualization has health benefits such as the lowering of blood pressure as well as the level of stress hormones in the blood. While that is all to the good, if it is true, what is useful here is that the technique can help to dampen down that wandering tendency of the untrained mind by providing a theme-based series of images that act like a railway track on which to carry your train of thought to an inner destination – W.B. Yeats' 'deep heart's core'. Let us now engage in some practical guided meditation exercises.

Visualizing

Some people can 'see' mental pictures better than others – these pictures are called 'eidetic' images. These are so vivid that it is like having an inner cinema. While not everyone is generously endowed with this mental capacity, most people can achieve some level of eidetic visualization if they keep working at it. For this reason, guided meditations with their visual descriptiveness can help the process. We visualize when we dream, or when we remember past scenes and events, so the equipment is there ready in our brains – it just needs polishing. One aid to this is to precede guided meditation sessions with several minutes of breath-focused exercises, ensuring that

'We visualize when we dream, or when we remember past scenes and events – the equipment in our brains just needs polishing.'

there is an even flow of air through *both* nostrils: experienced meditators claim that this helps to develop eidetic memories, and from this it is but a short step to being able to conjure up vivid mental images during meditation sessions.

Many people prefer someone to read out the guided narrative. The problem with this is timing – the speaker's speed might jar with your preferences. Reading and recording the sequential narrative yourself goes some way around this problem, but best of all is to learn the 'story' yourself, so the whole thing is self-generated imagination, and flexible. The sequences in the exercises are not overly complex and are easy to learn. They are like developing a disciplined form of the day-dreaming process. So, read the text of a guided narrative several times until you are thoroughly familiar with it – imprint it on the mind – before using it in meditation.

The length of time that a guided meditation lasts is basically up to you. The sequence of events or images does not have to happen in real time; some parts can be fairly briefly imagined, other parts you might dwell on longer. It depends on what you prefer or what you feel is necessary for a particular meditation. A general estimate for a guided meditation would be from ten to fifteen minutes overall, but I stress that is only a general possibility, and could be considerably briefer or much longer.

Picture this: guided meditations

This chapter contains guided visualization themes ranging from simple to more complex imagery – choose the one or ones that most appeal to you, or try them all. Remember that the best method, usually, is to mentally imprint the progression of imagery in a selected guided narrative sufficiently well to be able to follow it inwardly by yourself.

Our first exercise here focuses on the sky – an apt real-world metaphor for consciousness. Ground level is the mundane level of our busy, everyday state of mind. Above are clouds and thunderstorms acting like the jumble of thoughts, moods and concerns that obscure the sunlight and the endless blue sky beyond – an image analogous to the perfect 'clear-light mind' of Tibetan Buddhism. We all know what the sky looks like in its various moods, and many of us have flown high above the clouds, so this chapter's first guided meditation makes great use of memory images to help bolster our visualization efforts.

Let's fly.

EXERCISE 9

Taking wings

1. Adopt your chosen posture and breathe calmly. Quieten yourself, close your eyes and rein in your overactive mind. Focus.

2. Imagine that you are standing on the ground and above you is a sky full of grey clouds, moody and lowering. In the distance there are even darker clouds, periodically producing flashes of lightning. But more closely, here and there, occasional brief shafts of sunlight are poking through temporary breaks in the cloud cover.

3. You do not want to stay down here, so imagine yourself running forwards, feeling lighter and lighter until you gently leave the ground as if you had taken wings. You soar up into the grey cloudbase.

4. You continue to rise upwards through the dark clouds until you pass out of them into a region of brighter, whiter clouds, between which you catch glimpses of blue sky. Upwards, higher and higher you fly, feeling ever more weightless.

5. At last you break clear of all the clouds and they now lie beneath you, their tops gleaming white in the sunlight. You leave them further below as you climb up into the clear blue yonder. There is no wind here, it is empty blue sky, and you can fly freely in all directions. There are no boundaries, only the sun, the clear blue sky and you.

6. Stay here a while, free as a bird, before you allow yourself to slowly descend back through the clouds to land again on the ground.

There are other guided visualizations that also use meditation to encourage your consciousness to reach for higher levels with the help of appropriate imagery. One, like the next exercise, uses the literal image of ascending a mountain. This is a particularly powerful image: because of their spiritual symbolism, physical mountains were often selected as locations for the practice of meditation by ancient spiritual orders. For example, from the earliest times in Japan there was the tradition of the *gyo-ja*, the mountain ascetic. In the eighth century, Buddhism developed the 'nature wisdom school', whose adherents sought enlightenment by being close to nature in the mountains. Or, a world away, there was a sixth-century Celtic Christian monk called St Brynach, who would periodically feel drawn to meditate on a modest peak in the Preseli Hills of South Wales. It was believed that angels appeared to him on the summit, which accounts for the name of the hill, Carn Ingli – Welsh for 'Hill of Angels'. (Intriguingly, this rocky peak in Preseli possesses a strong magnetic anomaly – a compass needle will swing around to point South instead of North, sometimes even with the compass being held in mid-air.)

This association of mountains with spirituality is deeply embedded in the human psyche, which is why it is virtually a universal association. It is found even among Native American tribes. For instance, Ninaistákis ('Chief Mountain') in the Rocky Mountains of the northern US is sacred to the Blackfoot Indians. It dominates the landscape, standing a short distance from the main mountain mass. From one angle, the shape of its summit looks rather like a chief's topknot, while from another view it resembles a traditional upright headdress or bonnet. When the wind blows the mountain 'sings', due to many cracks and crevices in its summit rocks, and at sunrise and sunset it shines out and is visible for tens of miles in many directions. It was and is a place of traditional Blackfoot spiritual activity. High on its ridges and buttresses, and those of the surrounding mountains, both ancient and modern vision-questing sites are to be found. These take the form of small enclosures of rocks, just big enough to sit or lie in, or platforms of flat stones. Vision-questing structures oriented on Ninaistákis have been discovered up to 50 miles from the mountain and in locations up to 10,000 feet. Fortunately, we do not have to seek such extreme places for our purposes!

For the following exercise, you might find it helpful to find a stunning picture of some remote, snowy mountain peak, and dwell on it for five minutes or so. But then set it aside, close your eyes, and put on your mental climbing boots.

EXERCISE 10

Climbing the mountain

1. Imagine yourself climbing upwards towards the glacial wastes of a Himalayan peak. At first there is only the struggle of dealing with a steep, rocky slope. But when you clear the level of the clouds you find yourself surrounded by the crystal clarity of the light high above them.

2. As you scale ever upwards in your climb, you will sense your mind ascending higher, towards increasingly expansive states of consciousness.

3. When you reach the summit, experience what the late Sufi teacher, Pir Vilayat Inayat Khan, referred to as the 'cool transcendental light … of very high altitudes, almost frozen, immaculate and diaphanous.'

4. Spend time absorbing this high-altitude mental imagery. Here is the place for silent contemplation. Stay awhile. Consider the Zen saying: 'When you get to the top of the mountain, keep climbing.'

5. When ready, start your descent back to the base of the mountain.

We sometimes talk about 'going with the flow' with regard to life's events, by which we mean allowing things to unfold, being relaxed and not struggling. These are equally good maxims for setting up a mental frame for meditation. The next exercise perfectly incorporates that spirit. It is a guided visualization narrative that has various versions. It's time to go aboard …

EXERCISE 11

Going with the flow

1. Adopt your most comfortable posture, breathe calmly, close your eyes and then picture this: it is a perfect summer's afternoon, and you are in a rowing boat on a calmly flowing river. Lay down your oars and just lean back in the boat, allowing the river to carry the boat and you along. Trust the river's current. Relax.

2. As you float along, with your mind's eye look at the river banks on either side as you pass by. On the left, you see a clump of reeds, then a wise-looking old fisherman sitting on a rock with his fishing rod. He smiles at you as the river gently takes you onward. On the right, you can make out mountains, appearing blue in the distance, and a few weeping willow trees closer by. Continue looking left and right as you float along. What do you see, what scenes do you pass?

3. You are floating... floating along...

▶

4. You trust the river's flow with increasing confidence. You begin to notice that the river is becoming broader. Floating further along, you become aware that you are now in an increasing expanse of water, and you realize you are entering the river's estuary. The river is just about to merge into a calm, sunlit sea, taking you with it. You are floating free, safe inside the boat.

5. You are floating gently in the sunshine in the lapping, glittering water at the edge of the sea. Hold that image and stay with that sensation for a while.

6. The river has shared its journey with you, and taken you to where it was always going, just like the river of life. But you are not yet ready to float out further into the endless ocean, and it is time to end the meditation session, so mentally picture yourself picking up the oars again, and rowing steadily to a shore on one side or other of the estuary. Climb out of the rowing boat and open your eyes.

Other geographies of the mind

The previous three exercises provide the meditator with straightforward mental vectors. But the terrain of the mind, of the psyche, has a definite geography, and can be explored in other directions as well, using slightly more complex imagery, as the following two exercises demonstrate.

The first of these encourages the meditator to journey mentally inward into the deeper, darker recesses of the psyche instead of the lighter upward and flow vectors of consciousness, and demands an effort to imagine not only imagery but other senses too, as they are cued. So, prepare your posture and breathing as you usually do, close your eyes and settle down to follow the guided visualization.

EXERCISE 12

Going down to the woods

1. You are in dense woodland. You are walking down a fairly straight earthen woodland track. The foliage is thick around you and the branches of the trees arch over your head, making the path seem like a long, gloomy green tunnel.

2. You continue along the path… walking, walking.

3. The green gloom around you is both eerie and enticing, giving an aura of mystery. You almost feel as if you are in some kind of Grimms' fairy tale. You can smell the earth beneath your feet and the foliage around you as you walk.

4. As you progress along this living green tunnel through the heart of the woodland, you begin to notice trees on either side of the earthen path becoming festooned with strips of cloth. You recognize that these are votive offerings, indicating that a holy place must be only a short distance up ahead. Indeed, you can see a patch of pale light ahead of you at the end of the gloomy, green tunnel of trees. You approach it, closer and closer. Suddenly you emerge from the tunnel and you are standing in a woodland clearing. The sky is overcast, and it is early twilight.

5. In the middle of this clearing stands a tiny, ancient chapel with honey-coloured stone walls and a timber roof. You hear the tinkling sound of running water. You walk around the time-worn chapel and see golden, flickering light glimmering out of a narrow arched window and an open

▶

entrance. Next to the entrance there stands an old man, dressed in dark green robes. He smiles at you and gestures for you to enter the chapel. You go inside. The interior is lit by candles fixed at points around the walls. In one corner there is a large stone basin into which there is running a dribble of water from some hidden spring. It is this that is making the tinkling sound you heard. You walk over to the basin and look into the clear, gently shimmering pool of water it contains. This is an ancient, holy and healing fount, which many people have struggled to reach. Peer into the water – can you see your reflection in it?

6. Slowly slip your hands into the cool water. Turn them palms uppermost, then bring them out, dripping wet. Dab the cool moisture around your eyes and onto your lips.

7. Go over to the middle of the chapel floor, which is bare earth, and lie down. Watch the golden candlelight flickering on the interior of the golden stone walls and the roof timbers of the tiny chapel. You feel cosy and safe, and you begin to feel the healing effects of the water. You are feeling better and better. Stay in this sense of well-being for a little while.

8. Eventually, the old wise-looking monk in the dark green robes enters the chapel and indicates that it is time for you to leave. You get up and the old monk guides you back along the path that led you to the clearing.

9. You reach the edge of the woodland. The monk comes no further but waves you on your way. Open your eyes.

The next exercise is the final one in this chapter. It utilizes a powerful mental structure based on the Kabbalistic Tree of Life. As we learned in Chapter 1, the roots of Jewish mysticism are found in the philosophies of the Kabbalistic teachings. The Kabbalah is based on the Tree of Life cosmogram (a geometric figure depicting a cosmology; see opposite) which, read from top to bottom, represents the passage of energy from its pure spiritual state down into its final solid, physical form. Kether represents the crown centre; Malkuth corresponds to the seat of matter.

The tree consists of ten 'sephiroth', a Hebrew term meaning 'holy emanation'. They are connected by paths (and can also be referred to as branches). When depicted as a diagram on paper, the 'tree' appears as if on a single plane, but adepts believe that it operates on four separate levels or 'worlds'.

Among the meditative exercises associated with this particularly rich conceptualization is one called 'path-walking'. The meditator is required to conduct visualized journeys along the parts of the tree, between the various sephiroth. In this case, we will use a visualization that takes us path-waking to the central sephiroth of Tiphareth, which represents beauty.

Be respectful of the fact that you will be using a powerful cosmogram that is mapped deep in the subconscious mind.

Adopt your favoured posture, close your eyes and spend some minutes focusing on your breathing before you begin the visualization exercise overleaf.

'The Kabbalah represents the passage of energy from its pure spiritual state down into its final solid, physical form.'

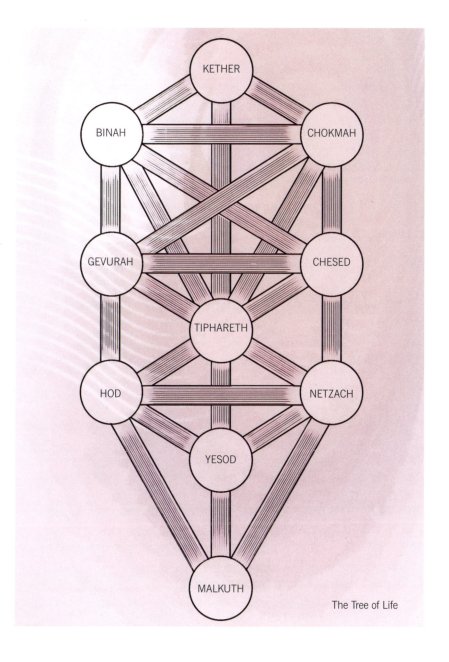

The Tree of Life

EXERCISE 13

The walled garden

1. You are in a walled garden, standing on a large green lawn, edged with flowers of many colours. The sun is directly overhead – it is high noon and you throw no shadow. Look at the walls of the garden. They are made of ancient-looking blocks of stone, golden yellow in colour, and are punctuated at various intervals by great wooden doors, with large black iron rings as handles. All the doors are closed.

2. As you look around, note that there are three barred doors in each of three walls, and a single barred door in the fourth wall. You walk over to one of the barred doors and try turning its great iron ring, but you cannot open the door.

▶

You try another door, but you cannot open that either. You realize that you cannot open any of these doors by yourself.

3. Without you being aware of it, a white-haired, white-robed man has walked across the lawn behind you and now stands beside you. He radiates compassion, and smiles at you. You silently understand that he will be your companion. He leads you towards one of the walls with three doors and opens the centre one. He signals for you to walk through.

4. A path stretches straight ahead of you. It is made of bright white flagstones that do not seem heavily worn. Look to your right and to your left as you walk along the path. You can see trees and flowers all around. Brightly coloured birds can be seen on tree branches, and flitting between the trees. As you walk along the straight white path, listen to the song of the birds and the contented hum of the bees. Feel the warmth of the sun on your body.

5. Walk on. With each step you feel more joyful. With each step you leave all your normal worries and fears and doubts further and further behind. You continue walking along the white straight path, among the flowers and trees, listening to the birdsong and the humming bees.

6. As you walk along, you see something glinting in the distance. You walk closer and closer towards it.

7. The path you are on comes to a great paved circle from which seven other white stone paths radiate in all directions, disappearing among the trees and flowers. In the centre of the white paved circle is a huge fountain. You slowly walk

▶

around it. It is a fantastic, carved stone structure from the top of which jet out great streamers of water. These jets of water arc up against the rich blue sky, then cascade back, wetting the stone structure as they return underground with a laughter-like sound through the openings around the stone base of the fountain. As you look up at this beautiful fountain, its waters sparkle in a myriad of colours. The droplets look like jewels as they shower down – here, you see a rich red ruby, there, glistening green droplets like emeralds, and everywhere are sparkling white diamond-like drops of water. As you walk around this fountain, you catch brief glimpses of soft rainbows in the watery mist.

8. You circle the fountain until you are back on the path along which you came. You know it is time to leave this wonderful place, but you know you will come again whenever you can. You walk back along the long straight white stone path, enjoying the sunlit surroundings, until you see the doorway in the walled garden ahead of you.

9. Your white-haired, white-robed companion, who you had forgotten has been silently following you, now overtakes you and opens the wooden door. You enter the walled garden, and watch your companion close the door. You thank him. He smiles at you and walks off out of sight behind you once more. As you stroll across the lawn, you gradually return to normal consciousness. You open your eyes, feeling happy and fulfilled.

Archetypes

You will have noticed the appearance of an image of an old, wise-looking man in three of this chapter's exercises: as a fisherman, he has smiled at you from the river bank; he has managed your time at a forest chapel; and he opened a door in a walled garden for you. This figure is what the famous and controversial Swiss psychologist, Carl Jung, called an 'archetype'. According to him, archetypes are 'primordial images', or active mental prototypes, residing deep in each person's psyche, waiting to be awakened – often in dreams, but also in age-old fairy tales, spontaneous visions and altered mind states like meditation. They exist in the unconscious mind in each of us because they are an extremely archaic inheritance from humanity's universal collective unconscious.

Archetypes are therefore simultaneously both personal and universal. The physical analogy is evolution – so, for example, the human hand is the product of untold generations of evolution, but can be used by an individual in manifold ways.

Jung identified a specific range of archetypal figures or images, and one of them is that of The Wise Old Man – sometimes referred to in the Jungian psychological literature as senex (Latin for 'old man'). He can sometimes appear in the guise of Teacher, Guru, Philosopher, Wizard and so forth. Similarly, the Wise Old Woman – sometimes Crone, Wise Witch, Great Mother and other guises. In these guided meditations this figure represents deep knowledge of the Self that is hidden from the conscious mind. It is, if you like, the 'invisible friend' of childhood translated into the companion of the adult seeker of wisdom. The archetype is always by your side, if a little behind you – you are not alone. Look for him in your dreams as well.

Moving on

If you regularly practise any or all of the guided meditations in this chapter, your ability to mentally visualize will become progressively stronger, and with practice will develop into almost cinematic clarity. When you are satisfied that you have achieved sufficient ability for your purposes, it is time to move to single-point meditation, as described in Chapter Six.

CHAPTER SIX

Single-point Meditation

·····································

Whatever comes to the eye,
Leave it be …

With empty mind really
Penetrated, the divine laws
Have no life.
When you can be like this,
You've completed
The ultimate attainment.

P'ang Yün (eighth-century Zen poem)

This more minimalist type of meditation focus requires a greater degree of mental discipline than following a stream of imagery in guided visualization. It is therefore advisable to have gained some experience with guided visualization before starting single-point meditation, which is analogous to carefully tuning a radio to find just one station – a clear signal among the noise. It requires sustained attention.

Several themes are described in this chapter. Try out each one to find which best suits you, because this is a demanding form of meditation. It is the ultimate way of quietening your consciousness, emptying your mind and mastering the ability to concentrate, to centre your consciousness. Powerful peace.

The mind's eye

In the course of this chapter, the exercises will take us from purely internal one-point visualization through to concentration on external objects.

First are inner imagery themes to test and develop your ability for one-pointed attention. Initially, you will probably not be able to hold your focus on a theme's single-point image for very long, but gently and repeatedly bring your inner eye back to it until you can hold it for an extended period of time. Precede each exercise with at least a five-minute session of breathing meditation, focusing only on the inhalation and exhalation of your breath.

'Single-point meditation is the ultimate way of quietening your consciousness, emptying your mind and mastering the ability to concentrate.'

The first exercise is one of two in this chapter that I owe to Professor Charles Laughlin, the neuroanthropologist I have mentioned a number of times, who underwent extensive initiation in Tibetan Buddhist dream yoga. The first of these exercises uses as the one-point visualized focus a bindu, a Sanskrit term meaning 'dot' or 'drop', representing in Hindu cosmology an elementary particle of prana, the all-pervading life force of the universe.

EXERCISE 14

To the point

1. Close your eyes. Lightly press the base of your throat, and immediately imagine a neon-like red point the size of a pea radiating with tremendous intensity at the place where you feel the light pressure of your finger. Remove your finger.

2. When you stabilize this mental image, start intoning an 'aahhh' sound very softly. Feel it resonating deep in your throat, in your larynx, where that intense, glowing red bindu is located. Gradually fade the 'aahhh' until you are intoning almost silently, even mentally.

3. Hold this imagery. Feel the bindu radiating in your throat.

4. Keep your mind empty and clear. Simply observe any arising associations, thoughts or images and let them pass. Keep to the point.

EXERCISE 15

Star bright

1. Breathing calmly and rhythmically, take up your favoured posture and close your eyes.
2. It is early twilight, and you are standing near the edge of a cliff looking across a wide valley that is filled with ever-deepening shadow. Alongside you on the cliff is a tiny wooden chapel, and huddled outside it sits an old, smiling monk, barely visible in the dwindling light. (This is the last time in this book you will read about this senex archetype, but that doesn't mean he won't be there in your other meditation sessions.)
3. The monk looks up at you and acknowledges you, then brings an arm out from under his robes and points across the valley. He is indicating a mountain with a single, sharp-pointed peak on the far side. Because of the distance across the valley, the mountain appears as a deep blue colour, silhouetted against the last glow of the fading sunset in the sky.
4. Just above the sharp point of the mountain peak gleams the evening star, shining steadily like a tiny lamp. No other stars are yet visible, just this brilliant dot of light. Focus all your attention on it, until you are no longer aware of the mountain peak, no longer aware of the valley, no longer aware of the temple and monk, and no longer aware even of yourself – only that shining star in a silent void of being.
5. Be still, and hold that focus for as long as you can, enjoying the quietude of your mind.

Outside in

Now to try a little mental alchemy. The mystics and great meditators tell us that 'all is One', that there is no outside nor inside. This is pretty much impossible for most of us to imagine, yet at least we can take it as a theme for the next two exercises, each based on one of the classic meditation practices – focusing on a candle flame. Laughlin reckons that the purpose of using an external focus is to ultimately internalize it as an eidetic image and let that become the focus of meditation.

EXERCISE 16

Guiding light
For this exercise you will need a candle, a candleholder and a lighter or box of matches.

1. Place a candle in an appropriate candleholder on a surface in front of where you are sitting. Ideally, nothing should be visible in the background that could divert your attention. A dark backdrop is best, and in any case the meditation space should be darkened. Also, be sure that the candle is not placed too near an open window or air source, such as a fan or heater, so that there is no danger of the flame burning too unsteadily or going out during the meditation session.
2. Taking all safety precautions, light the candle and assume a comfortable posture. Allow yourself to relax as you gaze at the candle's flame. Become totally absorbed in its gentle light. Focus on it single-pointedly.

▶

3. Try to reach a stage where nothing else exists in your mind except the flame. Become absorbed into its essence. Its essence is light.

4. Be still. Let your mind dwell peacefully in the light for as long as possible. Sense the vast expanse of your consciousness.

If your attention wavers during the previous exercise, return your focus gently and repeatedly to the flame at which you are gazing: use that glowing point of light as a leash to recall your wayward mind. If images or associations rise in your consciousness, let them pass like ships in the night. Simply observe them, then let them pass. The light is the guide.

Another way to use a candle flame meditation is to observe the effect of after-images (see Exercise 17, opposite). Although these are retinal effects, they can be used to enhance your inner visualizing abilities and can perhaps offer a shortcut to developing eidetic images if you are having difficulties in doing so.

Repeat this exercise at regular intervals – at least once a week. While a consistent light source like a candle flame is optimum, try varying the exercise by using the bright reflection from a metal or glass object.

'If images or associations rise in your consciousness, let them pass like ships in the night. The light is the guide.'

Keeping with the optical physiology, the next exercise is loosely based on the second Laughlin one in this chapter combined with insight from Buddhaghosa, who was an important fifth-century Indian Theravada Buddhist scholar. Theravada is a school of Buddhism that believes it stays closest to the actual teachings of the Buddha. This is a very sophisticated exercise, essentially inviting you to peer into the depths of your unconscious mind.

EXERCISE 17

Let the light in

For this exercise you will need a candle, a candleholder and a lighter or box of matches.

1. Be relaxed, comfortable and breathing calmly. Gaze upon the flame with calm but steady intensity for several minutes.

2. Close your eyes. Observe the after-image of the flame. Look into it and try to hold it steady. It may slowly change colour, or even become a negative image before it fades, perhaps with a sliding motion if you are not holding your closed eyes very steady.

3. When the after-image finally fades away, open your eyes and gaze again upon the actual candle flame. Do so for several minutes, before again closing your eyes and calmly observing the after-image once more. Be aware that a perception of the candle flame is now inside you, in front of your mind's eye.

4. Repeat this process three or four times, trying to become increasingly more adept at extending the life of the after-image, and closely examining its nature. Play with it.

5. Finally, extinguish the actual candle flame. Remain in the darkened meditation space with your eyes closed and try to visualize the after-image of the candle flame.

EXERCISE 18

What lies beneath
For this exercise you will need a medium-grey bowl.

1. Take a medium-grey bowl, as large as possible, and fill it with clear water almost to the brim. Place it a few feet away from you and at an angle below your eye level. Sit in a relaxed, comfortable posture and either gaze down into the water in the bowl or at any reflections on its surface. Gaze without distraction into the water for at least five minutes. Gaze deeply.

2. Then, interrupt your gaze into the water by closing your eyes at short intervals, trying to picture the water with your mind's eye. Repeat until you can hold an inner image of the water reasonably effectively.

3. Then remove the bowl and water, settle in a comfortable position again, close your eyes and maintain sustained concentration on the inner image, and think only of the nature of water.

4. Look into that image – what do you discern? What is happening beneath the surface? Without making a conscious effort, apply patience and wait until forms literally 'bubble up' spontaneously from within your inner image of the water. You might see watery things such as bubbles or currents moving lazily within the water, you may see moving reflections on the water, or you may see a mist rising above it. But traditional

▶

imagery may also spontaneously arise – archetypal symbols or other content from the depths of the collective unconscious: the ancient texts of Buddhaghosa mention the possible appearance of a crystalline form, while Laughlin refers to a 'crystalline network'.

Observe, and go where the imagery takes you.

In the Buddhaghosa texts, images arising in meditation similar to this exercise are referred to as 'signs'. Among others, he describes 'stars', 'clusters of gems or pearls', 'a puff of smoke' and the 'moon's disc'.

Inside out

The term 'mandala' is Sanskrit for 'circle', and it is used widely as a meditation device in Hindu and Buddhist practice in particular, but also from antiquity in other religions and cultures around the world.

Essentially, a mandala is a visual device consisting of a circle with a centre point, though the circle can itself often be placed within a square, which is, typically, quartered or even has a grid superimposed on it.

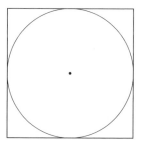

This basic structure is usually hugely elaborated upon with a rich variety of symbolic religious imagery to produce a very intricate, multicoloured and beautiful overall visual effect (see below), very meaningful to the relevant religious adherents.

In general Hindu and Buddhist terms, the mandala represents the universe, though in modern western thought it is widely felt to represent psychological wholeness. As Carl Jung wrote in *Memories, Dreams, Reflections*: 'I sketched every morning in a notebook a small circular drawing ... which seemed to correspond to my inner situation at the time. ... Only gradually did I discover what the mandala really is: ... the Self, the wholeness of the personality, which if all goes well is harmonious.'

The origins of the mandala image are unknown, but archaeologists have uncovered mandala-like markings many thousands of years old. Jung was sure that the mandala originated spontaneously in the human collective unconscious, in dreams, visions and other altered mind states, thus accounting for its timeless universality. This 'deep mind' origin is why the mandala is such a prime tool for meditation.

Mandalas can be produced in many ways: drawn or painted in bright colours on paper or fabric scrolls (called *tankas* in Tibet), or laid out in coloured sands or rice, among many other means of depiction which nowadays include computer graphics.

In Tibetan Buddhism there is a method known as *dykil-'khor*, which consists of constructing a mandalic form with rice on a round metallic surface, then wiping the surface clean and repeating the process. The special bowl used for this procedure is called a *sa-gzhi* in Tibetan and is made of silver or copper with symbolic engravings and often with a gold inlay around the rim. It is used upside down, and its base consists of a flat, matte-finished surface upon which the rice mandala is created. Over three months at a Tibetan retreat, Laughlin achieved the initiatory requirements of producing one hundred thousand rice mandalas. The process required concentrated, rapid activity. Laughlin found that once this demanding process had got underway he would have powerful, lucid dreams almost every night. (Lucid dreams are those in which one becomes fully conscious inside a dream while remaining physiologically asleep.) The dreams were all mandalic in some way, having circular peripheries around dynamic centres through which Laughlin could sometimes glimpse scenes.

But on a whole other scale, there are also architectural ways of constructing mandalas. In Hindu towns the central temple represented Mount Meru, a mythical mountain whose physical embodiment is Mount Kailash in the Himalayas, sacred to Hindus and Buddhists alike. In Hindu cosmology, Meru is the mythical centre of the world. Eighteenth-century Jaipur was built according to this traditional model – in effect, the symbolism was actually lived out by the city's inhabitants.

The symbolic image of the North Star (Polaris, the Pole Star) shining above the peak of mythological Mount Meru represents the fulcrum in Hindu (and earlier) cosmology – the combined image is the still centre around which the universe turns, and can also represent the focused 'centring' of one's consciousness. (This is the essence, of course, of the Star Bright exercise earlier in this chapter.) This combined symbolic image was actually architecturally created in the fourteenth century at the ancient Indian city of Vijayanagara, about 200 miles south-west of Hyderabad. Now ruinous, it was once one of the largest cities in the world, the capital of a great Hindu empire. It was laid out on a mandalic plan and, standing at a ceremonial gateway looking north along the main north-south axis of the royal city, the eye is led to the Virabhadra temple on the summit of Matanga Hill. John McKim Malville and John Fritz, who researched the layout of the city, saw the Pole Star shining above the temple. Thus they realized that the architecture of the city combined with the layout of the landscape cleverly recreated a localized version of this symbolic image.

Angkor Wat, the famous temple in Cambodia, a Khmer masterpiece, also architecturally acknowledges the mandalic form and represents Mount Meru. It was originally constructed as a Hindu temple dedicated to the god Vishnu, but was gradually transformed into a Buddhist temple towards the end of the twelfth century. It is comprised of massive architecture covered in finely detailed carvings and reliefs. The five central towers (stupas) of Angkor Wat represent the peaks of Mount Meru. The outer wall around the temple represents the mountains of the edge of the world, and the moat beyond represents the cosmic ocean in which the world floats. Its ground plan is mandalic. Elsewhere in the vast Angkor complex, other temples symbolize the same cosmological model.

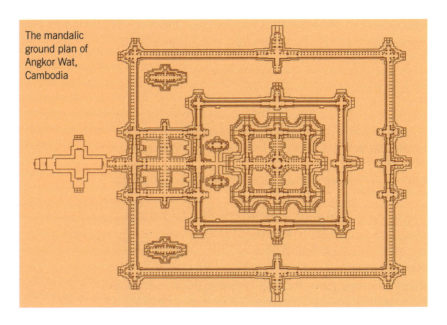

The mandalic ground plan of Angkor Wat, Cambodia

The ground plan of Borobudur as a mandala

Another superb example expressing a similar mandalic symbolism is the Buddhist temple of Borobudur, which also stands on an earlier Hindu site in Central Java, Indonesia. A vast hilltop construction, it dates from about 900 CE. It boasts nearly two miles of stone-worked panels depicting Buddhist teachings and legends and almost 1,500 lattice stupas, plus some 500 life-size seated statues of the Buddha. The temple consists of nine superimposed terraces reducing in size upwards, and the whole is crowned by a huge, bell-shaped stupa. From above, it appears as a three-dimensional mandala. Borobudur is meditation made physical and, indeed, it has been described as 'a prayer in stone'.

For our purposes, the following meditation exercise uses just a 'bare bones' version of the mandala. It is the ultimate single-point challenge – it leaves you with nowhere else to go.

EXERCISE 19

At the centre of the self

For this exercise you will need some paper, a pair of compasses and a pencil.

1. Using a pair of compasses, draw a circle and mark the centre with a small dot –the bindu. (As a trial exercise, use the figure in this book, although a larger circle is advised for more engaged meditation sessions.) Fix the drawing vertically, with the central dot at eye level. Settle in your favoured, most comfortable posture, breathe calmly and evenly, then focus on the dot.

2. As you gaze at the dot, be aware of the circle in your peripheral vision but don't look at it directly. Consider the circle to be the Self, your Self, and the dot the deep centre, the bindu, of your consciousness.

3. Do not distract your gaze from the dot – maintain a long, undivided and absorbed focus on it. Allow it to totally centre your awareness. As you do so, contemplate the nature of your Self, existing beyond time and space behind the socially defined person you think you are in everyday life. Who are you really?

4. All the time your attention is absorbed by the dot, realize that you are greater than your mundane self, greater than your physical body, that your deep essence is ageless, beyond death. Hold this combined visual focus and mindful contemplation for as long as possible, and for at least ten minutes.

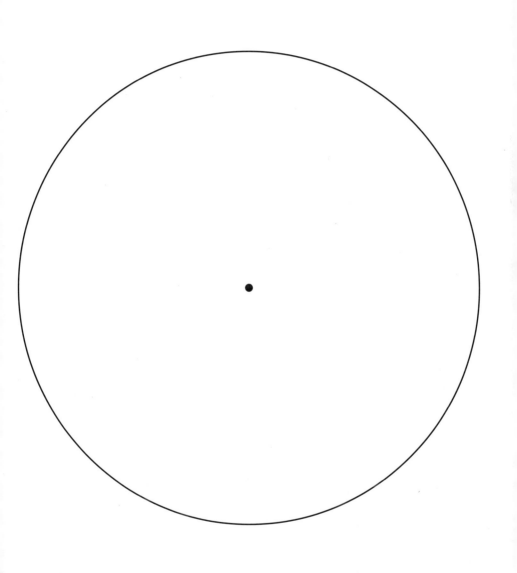

You can also try this exercise using more complex circular geometry, such as concentric circles, but use only a few, well-spaced nested circles, narrowing towards the outer edge (such as in the illustration below), to avoid the appearance of a tunnel. In this case, centre your consciousness inside the space of the centre circle.

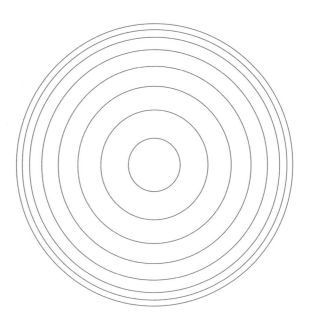

'Contemplate the nature of your Self,
existing beyond time and space.
Who are you really?'

Yantra

Traditionally used as a tool for votive meditation, a yantra is a kind of specialized mandala, a mystical diagram, and can sometimes occupy the central part of a mandala. A yantra is dedicated to a particular deity and will have several geometric shapes radiating concentrically from the centre – interlocking triangles (the Sri Yantra – see below) being a key favoured visual device. This central geometry is often enclosed by a square representing the four cardinal directions, with doors to each of them. It is said by some that deep, sustained concentration on the central visual device of a yantra, perhaps while intoning a relevant mantra, can cause the meditator to briefly glimpse the spectral form of the venerated deity emerging from the geometry.

The Sri Yantra

CHAPTER SEVEN

The Powers of Sound, Light and Nature

There is a rapture on the lonely shore,
There is society where none intrudes,
By the deep Sea, and music in its roar:
I love not Man the less, but Nature more...

Lord Byron, '*Childe Harold's Pilgrimage*'

Although most of your meditation sessions will probably take place in your prepared space indoors, there might be times when you will want to meditate in the open air, in closer contact with nature. You may take part in organized meditation retreats, or have your own private quiet places for this purpose, perhaps a garden, yard or lawn, beach or little-visited corner of the local countryside. All these are good, but this chapter invites you to – on occasion – think more deeply about where you might have a meditation session in locations where Mother Nature can lend a hand to the meditator.

Because meditation is an inner mental process it is often overlooked that it can be encouraged by certain natural environmental factors. A sensory stimulus, such as the use of incense, is a well-known aid to meditation as we have already noted, but there are others as well, particularly certain kinds of sound and light in nature. The mind rides on the shoulders of the brain, after all, and the right kind of sensory environment can make it considerably easier to establish a meditational state of mind.

In his 2018 paper, Laughlin states that 'meditating upon auditory objects is mediated by a different entrainment of networks' in the brain than is apparently the case with visual or other objects of meditative focus. First of all, then, let us consider certain broad-frequency, background sounds in nature.

The colours of sound

Scientists refer to 'colours' of noise. There is white, pink, grey, red/brown and violet noise, and more, all with their specific energy distribution properties. For meditation purposes we are interested in white, pink and brown noise.

○ *White noise*

Usually thought of as the static hiss of an untuned radio, this contains all the sound frequencies audible to humans (roughly 20 to 20,000 hertz); its energy, or to put that more technically, signal power per hertz (hertz – cycle per second), is distributed equally across all the frequencies. It is analogous to white light, which is a combination of all the colour wavelengths. The roar of a large nearby waterfall is white noise.

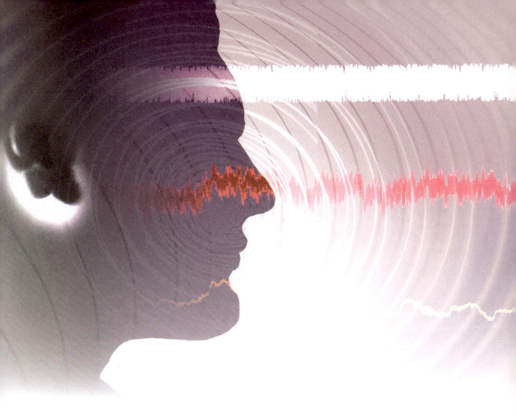

○ *Pink noise*

This has the same wide, random range of audible frequencies as white noise, but its power decreases as the frequency increases. Consequently, the lower frequencies are louder than the higher frequencies. Unlike white noise, pink noise distributes its power evenly across octaves (the doubling of frequencies) rather than frequencies. The architecture of the human ear is such that we hear sound in octaves, and pink noise is perceived as being smoother and more relaxing than white noise. It can be found in nature in the sound of rain falling on foliage, or gentle waves breaking on the beach.

○ *Brown noise*

The power of this quality of sound is based more on the lower frequency range than is pink noise. It can occur in nature as an even wind, especially when blowing through trees. A sonic breeze.

The science of sonic colours is more complex than all this, and involves factors such as pitch, but these are the basics as far as we are concerned here. There are research claims that immersion in these three kinds of sound can, variously, improve relaxation, sleep, concentration and even memory but, again, this is outside our immediate frame of reference.

So, natural background sounds can be taken into account when deciding where to meditate out of doors. But if you live in a city, as most of us do, an ideal place with suitable sonics is probably not readily accessible – not often, at any rate. There are two ways to overcome this: treat yourself to a 'meditation away-day' at such a location, and not only meditate while there but also record the sound, so you can use it later in your home; or purchase commercially available recordings of natural sounds. Also, on the Internet, there are freely available extensive recordings of white, pink and brown noise (see Resources at the end of this book).

Using nature's sounds for meditation

Let's take a large waterfall's roaring white noise as an example – interestingly, waterfalls are favoured by some indigenous people even today as places for initiation rituals. I call this exercise 'The Vasudeva Effect' (see page 111), named after the wise old ferryman in Herman Hesse's wonderful book, *Siddhartha*. In this, Siddhartha, exhausted and despondent after being on a failed spiritual quest for many years, stays with an old ferryman sage called Vasudeva. One day, when the two men are returning from taking a traveller across the river, the old man invites Siddhartha to pay close attention to the sound of the water flowing vigorously beneath them. Siddhartha does so, and in the roar of the river gradually discerns its 'many-voiced song'. It laughs and cries. Its voice becomes full of longing, then full of woe. Good and evil voices, voices of pleasure and sorrow, sounds of laughing and lamenting, voices of men, women and children. As he listens, he eventually hears all these noises coalesce into one great interwoven tapestry of sound: he realizes that the river is singing just one great song of life. In Hesse's book, Siddhartha's sense of self merges with the great sound of the river and becomes one with it. He experiences enlightenment.

While the following exercise might not transform us into a Buddha, it is nevertheless an interesting type of meditation session to conduct.

EXERCISE 20

The Vasudeva effect

1. Settle yourself down in your most comfortable meditation posture, breathe rhythmically and calm your mind.
2. Now, with your eyes closed, focus your attention on the sound of the waterfall. Allow your mind to gradually merge with it. After several minutes you may begin to hear various beats within the sound that result from the specific location of the waterfall: the way the waters are striking rocks, and the way the rock walls are reverberating with the sound. This is the signature of the place; the waters are telling you their story.

▶

3. Remain attentive, listening to the sounds. Soon, you might catch what seem to be voices calling from out of the roaring waters. A name is called. Perhaps your name, perhaps the name of a relative or friend; quite often, and curiously, it could be the name of someone you knew who has died.

4. The sound of the waterfall will now start telling you your story. Do not edit or resist what you hear – just let the white sound of the waters speak. If you allow, it will take you on a journey of deep introspection.

Now it's time to try a pink noise meditation (see Exercise 21, opposite), evoking Byron's 'By the deep Sea, and music in its roar'.

'Allow your mind to gently merge into the rhythm of the sea, and let your consciousness float beyond this time and place ...'

EXERCISE 21

Surf's up

1. Find an empty beach, perhaps out of season, when the sea is a little rougher and waves crash on to the sand. Sit well back from the sea and make yourself comfortable but with your back erect, as always.

2. Close your eyes, engage with your favoured breathing meditation and listen to the sound of the surf. Hear it variously murmur and roar as it comes and goes against the beach. Focus on your breathing while listening to the ceaseless voice of the sea.

3. Allow your mind to gently merge into its rhythm and absorb its wisdom, telling you about time and tide, about the cycles of heaven, the turning of the ages. Let your consciousness float beyond this time and place.

The ancient Greeks made use of nature's sounds at their oracle temples; this was usually the sound of roaring water, but sometimes it was the sound of wind blowing against the leaves of a tree. Dodona was one such example. The ruins of this oracle temple stand near the foot of Mount Tomaros. It was claimed that Zeus spoke through a sacred and 'voiceful' oak tree. It seems that it was the rustling sound made by wind blowing through the tree's foliage that was assumed to be the god's voice. The sound was interpreted by priests and priestesses as being Zeus's answer to questions put to the tree by petitioners. (The murmuring of a spring or fountain at the temple and a 'sounding brass' were other forms of sonic oracles at Dodona.)

The sound of the wind in foliage is sometimes pink and sometimes brown noise, depending on the density of the foliage and the strength of the wind, and either can be exploited by the meditator.

EXERCISE 22

Choose your own oracle

1. Select a place close to, but not in, a stand of trees – if deciduous it has to be a season when they have leaves, of course, but evergreens such as pine trees are especially effective for this exercise.
2. Listen openly to the wind in the trees, and focus your meditation on some deeply meaningful question, such as the nature of consciousness, or what is the Self.
3. Listen to the trees…

Echoes

Another type of sound that nature can provide is the echo. The Tuvan throat-singers of the steppes and mountains of the Tuva Republic (federated with Russia) provide a fine example of the use of echoes. Tuvan throat-singing originally developed as a means of communicating with the natural environment, rather than for entertainment. Throat-singing involves the production of resonance sounds, overtones and whistles within the throat, nasal cavities, mouth and lips, and was used to provoke echoes or imitate natural sounds such as waterfalls and wind. The master throat-singers select precise locations inside caves or in front of cliff faces, where the resonances are exactly right to maximize the reverberations of their songs. They even wait until the atmospheric conditions are perfect for the greatest effect. At one locale, where a throat-singer called Kaigal-ool performed in front of a cliff face, ethnomusicologist Theodore Levin observed that 'the cliff and surrounding features sing back to the musician in what Kaigal-ool calls "a kind of meditation – a conversation that I have with nature"'.

If you are feeling adventurous, do some research and take a meditation away-day to some safe but strongly echoing place – inside a cave (best option), facing a cliff face, on the floor of a narrow rocky canyon or gorge, in a place with rocky outcrops or by a small body of water surrounded by rocks or cliffs.

In the next exercise, make an effort to suspend your modern knowledge that an echo is the result of an initial sound, which is a pressure wave in the air that reflects back from a hard surface, and think about echoes more in the way that ancient people did – that they were the voices of spirits living within or behind rock surfaces. Echo phenomena surely lie at the heart of these kinds of beliefs. Algonquin Indians considered the foot of cliffs that rise out of water to be favoured haunts of the spirits, known as manitous, which is interesting because such locations are also particularly effective in the production of echoes – the water surface acts as a kind of amplifier and transmitter. An Algonquin shaman would mark such places as the abodes of spirits with rock art or simply a daub of red ochre, and would go into trance and send his out-of-body soul through cracks in rock surfaces to obtain 'rock medicine' (supernatural power) from the spirits within the rocks. Similar beliefs that a spirit world existed behind rock surfaces and cliff faces were held by many American Indian peoples and other peoples around the world, such as the San (Bushmen) in Southern Africa. So, temporarily, try to get into that former, pre-modern mindset. Inhabit it during your meditation session. It is surprisingly easy to do that if you select a strongly echoing place.

EXERCISE 23

Genius loci – spirit of place

1. Settle yourself in your chosen echo location. To ensure you select somewhere with strong or at least effective echoes, you can first test the sound-reflecting quality of a place simply by clapping your hands and listening. If it is difficult to sit comfortably in the locale, consider the use of a foldable canvas camping chair or stool.

2. First of all, sit with your eyes closed and simply listen to the place for several minutes. Wind noise may exist, or, in a cave, there may be the occasional 'plinking' sound of water dripping from a stalactite or, even, relative silence.

3. Then, after this familiarization, hold your head upwards and utter a mantra in as loud a voice as you can muster. The mantra can be one of your choosing but make it a simple one. A straightforward 'Om/Aum' would be ideal. Project the sound and make it a long, drawn-out one. Listen for the echo. You might have to experiment with loudness, pitch, timbre and projected direction to get the best result from your particular location.

4. When you have the optimum results, keep your eyes closed, utter your mantra at periodic intervals that seem right to you and listen to the echo. Think of it not as an echo in today's scientific sense, but as the spirit of the place, the genius loci, speaking. Set up a mythic connection with it. Give your modern cultural worldview a rest.

Light

Sunlight and fire in certain contexts can aid in encouraging meditative states of consciousness – but be warned that if you suffer from photosensitive epilepsy it would be best to ignore the following exercises because they involve optical flicker.

'Observe the sunlight sparkling and glinting on the wind-whipped wavelets on the water's surface, and see the moving, dazzling patterns.'

EXERCISE 24

Light fantastic

1. Find a position looking out across a large body of water, preferably the ocean, on a sunny day when a gentle-to-moderate breeze is blowing.

2. Start your breathing meditation but this time with your eyes open so you can observe the sunlight sparkling and glinting on the wind-whipped wavelets on the water's surface, and see the moving, dazzling patterns. That shimmer, combined with the concentration on your breathing, will soon induce relaxation, and before

▶

long a state of reverie, possibly due to the flicker of the glittering reflected sunlight entraining your brainwaves into alpha frequencies, or even light theta. The risk here is that the session might descend into drowsiness and an inadvertent nap, so it is important to keep an alert focus on the inhalation and exhalation of your breath.

3. If you can hear the sound of the surf as well, it will be an exceptional environment for promoting meditation. But, again, guard against drifting off to sleep!

Even if you (hopefully) maintain sufficient mental discipline to avoid falling asleep, the above conditions will almost inevitably take you to the borderlands of sleep, and you may experience hypnogogic imagery – those pictures and sounds that can flash momentarily into your mind just before you fall asleep. If you can manage to maintain control in the hypnogogic phase and slow it down (which requires some practice), an intriguing level of meditation can be experienced, with exceptionally vivid pictures and voice fragments rising up from the unconscious mind. Be on the lookout for the occasional flotsam of archetypal imagery.

Other natural optical flicker effects exist, of course. One example is sunlight streaming through windblown foliage in a forest environment throwing rapidly moving shadows over closed eyelids. This can also be explored, but it is a less reliable method and it is usually more difficult to set up a workable meditation session in such conditions. Another example is the dance of flames – a blazing fire in the hearth, if you have one, or a bonfire in the open air. The fiery flicker works on either open or closed eyes, and it is relatively easy to set up a meditation session in conjunction with the effect – again, using it as an adjunct to breathing meditation.

The counterpoint exercise to this is to use eyes-open breathing meditation with the embers of the fire as a visual focus. Peer into the deep red and orange glowing shapes and see the shifting repertoire of landscapes, castles and faces come and go as the embers burn down. If your meditative state deepens sufficiently, you might see increasing detail in the complexity of the glowing embers, and even perceive what appear to be tiny movies wrought in fire. But this exercise can become soporific, so once again falling asleep needs to be guarded against.

Fire-based sessions tap into what we might call cellular memory, dating back to when humans first mastered fire. It is an archetypal playground.

Tides of the day

In Old Europe and Scandinavia, there used to be a system of dividing up every twenty-four hours into eight three-hour periods, which were referred to as 'tides'. Each one of these was symbolically associated with a compass direction and a range of physical or mental conditions. (In this regard, the 'tides' are vaguely similar in purpose to Indian *ragas*, musical improvisations that have symbolic associations with season, time and mood.)

Here, with regard to meditation, we are concerned only with eventide and morntide, and the distinctive and evocative light associated with those times of day.

EXERCISE 25

Sunset meditation

1. Position yourself so that you are in your favoured posture and facing west, with open eyes. Engage in your accustomed breathing meditation. Start at least ten minutes before the sun begins to sink below the horizon. The traditional associations with eventide are joy and spirituality – it is literally a soulful time of day.

2. Keep these qualities in your mind as you conduct your breathing rhythms and watch the sunset and the glorious colours filling the western sky. Irish mythology tells that the Land of the Blessed, Tír na nÓg, lies just below the western horizon. If you are in a location with an ocean or other body of water in front of you, the setting sun will light a shining path across the water to that beatific place beyond.

3. Watch as the sunset colours in the evening sky start to fade and the world deepens into twilight: to use an old-fashioned but expressive word, it is the 'gloaming', a short period that has been referred to as 'the crack between the worlds'.

4. Close your eyes now. In tune with the quietening world around you, be still. Breathe.

The next exercise perhaps requires more of an effort or commitment than its counterpart at the end of the day, but it is worth it, at least occasionally.

EXERCISE 26

At the gates of dawn

1. Position yourself so that you are in your favoured posture and facing east, with open eyes. Engage in your accustomed breathing meditation.

2. Start at least an hour before sunrise (check the newspaper or online for the time of sunrise in your part of the world). Observe calmly as the sky softly lightens in the east. Carry the sense in your mind of coming out of darkness into light. Morntide has the traditional association of 'arousing'. Listen to the dawn chorus of the birds.

3. Watch for the first gleam of sunlight to flash out on the horizon, and then observe the glory of the rising sun. See it roll upward into the sky. Close your eyes and let the bright new sunlight shine on your closed eyelids. Breathe in the morning air and sense the world around you beginning to awaken.

4. Close the session about ten minutes after the sun has risen. Open your eyes. Arise and meet your new day.

If or when you decide to meditate out of doors, try as often as is practical to choose places and conditions of sound or light that will enhance your experiences. Let external nature meet your mind through the medium of meditation. It can add a whole other dimension that is hard to define but is no less real for all that.

CHAPTER EIGHT

The Power of Silence

There is a voice that doesn't use words. Listen.

The quieter you become the more you are able to hear.

Quotations from Rumi, thirteenth-century Sufi mystic

In contrast to the use of sound, silence can be a powerful aid for the practice of meditation – perhaps the most powerful of all. But with regard to meditation there are two types of silence: what we might call mundane silence, our normal everyday idea of it; and spiritual silence, a very deep state of consciousness that is the goal of those who undertake meditation primarily for spiritual betterment rather than purely for physical and mental well-being.

Mundane silence

In today's noisy world true silence is hard to come by. In urban or semi-urban areas there is a kind of background sound that most of us nowadays 'tune out' and mistake for silence. The birds know this: various research studies have shown that since the 1970s birdsong in cities has become louder and more high-pitched to cope with a gradual increase in the background 'hum'. Even out in the seemingly quiet country-side there can usually be the distant sound of an aircraft, train or traffic. Although, again, our ears may tune out such background sounds, an outdoor audio recording of a rural location can often surprise us!

While laboratory conditions can be configured to create conditions of absolute silence, in nature deep silence can usually only be obtained in deserts, polar regions and extremely remote places. Deserts were chosen by religious ascetics precisely because of their silence, and in remote northern regions such as Northern Karelia in eastern Finland there is now 'silence tourism'. As one Finnish tourist company puts it, deep silence gives the opportunity to escape from our loud modern world for a while and to 'listen to and concentrate on the rich nuances of silence, and to hear one's own mind'. That's pretty much a description of an ideal environment for meditation.

There has been insufficient research into how silence affects living organisms, but what has been done indicates that it can have specific positive effects, as a brief, random look at a few examples of scientific papers shows. A 2015 report of a study by Imki Kirste and colleagues on adult mice found that two hours of total silence per day led to the development of new cells in the hippocampus, an area of the brain associated with learning, memory and emotion. Studies on humans have yet to be carried out but it is hoped that these might determine that total silence could prove therapeutic for conditions such as depression and Alzheimer's, which are associated with reduced rates of neuron regeneration in the hippocampus. Work on human subjects by Dr Luciano Bernardi and colleagues in 2005 found that as little as two minutes of silence is more relaxing than listening to calming music, according to measurements of cardiovascular and respiratory changes and blood circulation in the brain. Another study, by Dr Joseph Moran and colleagues, showed that even in the idling, daydreaming or 'default mode network' state of brain function there is still activity going on regarding the internalizing and evaluating of information. Silence is found to amplify this process of self-reflection.

In short, it would seem that silence truly is golden.

These wider considerations aside, we need to make our home meditation space as quiet as possible, of course; but however successful we are, 'quiet' is unlikely to be quite the same as truly 'silent'. Even so, unless you are planning to be a desert ascetic or an Arctic shaman, you simply have to do your best to find as quiet a place as possible for your session. Soundproofing your meditation space could be one rather extreme and not necessarily practical answer, but another more accessible option that usually helps is timing: it is best to hold your daily meditation session in the very early morning hours before the world fully awakes, or in the late evening, when things wind down.

But all this is to do with mundane silence. For the person using meditation mainly as part of a spiritual journey, it is the treasure of inner silence that is being sought.

'Silence is found to amplify the process of self-reflection. In short, it would seem that silence truly is golden.'

Spiritual silence

What some mystics call the 'Silence' is the most exalted state of meditation. In the Christian Bible it is described as 'the peace of God, which passeth all understanding' (Philippians 4:7). It is not normal silence but an extremely deep altered state of consciousness that contains all sound, like bees in amber. It is behind and between all sounds. As the musicological therapist David Aldridge has put it, 'Silence is the core of music'.

The Silence is probably akin to the state of samadhi known to Buddhist, Hindu and yoga adepts, because in this most profound state of meditational absorption there is blissful freedom from the tyranny of time. No past, no future, which are simply memories and mental projections respectively. There really is just here and now, often referred to in spiritual literature as the 'Eternal Now'. The neuroanthropologist and advanced meditator, Charles Laughlin, calls this instant moment an 'epoch'. 'Normal, common sense experience is really a perceptual operation of binding the present epoch with memory of those that have gone just before the "now" moment and those that are anticipated to arise just after the "now" moment,' he writes in *Communing with the Gods*. He states that skilled contemplatives can slow down and clear their minds to the point where they can actually discern these 'epochs' as they arise.

'Sound is to the Silence what time is to eternity.'

Sound into silence

Ironically, the use of sound can lead the mind towards the Silence, as the following two exercises indicate.

EXERCISE 27

Listen to the resonance

For this exercise you will need a Tibetan (or Tibetan-style) singing bowl, something to stand it on and a wooden baton.

1. Adopt your favoured posture, your spine upright, as always. Place in front of you, on the floor or a low table, a Tibetan (or Tibetan-style) singing bowl and a wooden baton. The bowl should be placed on a small, soft stand to maximize resonance. Close your eyes and begin your breathing meditation. With every inhalation and exhalation meditate solely, single-mindedly, on this profound thought: Sound is to the Silence what time is to eternity.

2. Let the meaning of this enter deeply into your consciousness.

3. After several minutes of this, open your eyes. Strike the rim of the bowl firmly with the baton. Close your eyes again and follow the strong resonant ringing tone with your mind as it very gradually dissolves into silence. Follow every last vestige of the sound. This is a most calming and centring process.

4. Repeat several times, then, with eyes closed, after your final strike of the bowl, abide in the silence that the ringing sound has led you into. As the sound has done, dissolve into it. Meditate on the nature of eternity, which is not endless linear time – which is not time at all, in fact.

Another exercise using sound that lends itself to attainment of the Silence is the use of mantras, which we have previously discussed.

In meditation, the vocal sound of a mantra is ultimately internalized to become a mental, soundless resonance, acting as a kind of 'wave guide' for the meditator's consciousness as it reaches for deeper levels.

EXERCISE 28

The soundless sound

1. Settle yourself comfortably in your meditation posture. Establish your breathing pattern. Make the traditional Tibetan mantra sound, 'om' (pronounced as a long, drawn-out 'ohm'.)

2. Spend about five minutes repetitively uttering the sound out loud.

3. Spend the next five minutes repetitively uttering the sound in as low a vocal register as you can manage. Focus on the vibration in your throat as you recite the word.

4. Spend the next ten minutes repeating the mantra silently, purely as a mental process. Then be still and silent. Sense the soundless sound of the mantra.

Clearing the mind

There is no quick and easy way into the Silence, although Zen Buddhism offers what on the surface seems to be a quick method – the koan, a logic-stopping question or statement. A well-known example is 'What is the sound of one hand clapping?' The aspirant is to keep the koan constantly in his mind, no matter what he is doing. Theoretically, when the koan finally exhausts his logical way of thinking, the aspirant's usual mental processes are momentarily halted, and like a door in a prison being briefly opened, his mind can escape into a state beyond logical, linear thought, and he attains samadhi. In Zen terms, samadhi is a state of oneness in which the distinctions between things dissolve – the mind state that is beyond linear logic: namely, the Silence.

Zen literature gives many examples of monks who, when confronted with a koan put to them by a Zen Master, suddenly become enlightened, but it should be remembered that each monk may have spent years in stern, disciplined meditation so was ripe for the fleeting moment of insight: as the Zen adage says, 'A split hair's breadth and heaven and Earth are set apart'. The Master sees in his pupil when that split-hair

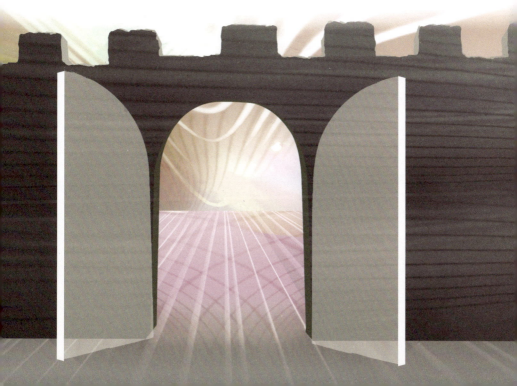

moment is imminent and deploys the koan as a final push. In Zen philosophy, it isn't really a question of gaining enlightenment, the Silence, samadhi, the Void, or whatever we choose to call it, because we are already enlightened; it is simply that we don't know it. The function of meditation is to remove the obstructions blocking the radiance of the Clear-Light Mind shining beyond time in the Silence.

Over the centuries various traditions involving the use of koans have evolved, such as in the context of interactions between Master and pupil, or in parable form, or as objects of introspection. The exercise below is in that latter form.

The use of a koan can stop that incessant internal mental chatter. It is like quietening the wind that ripples the surface of water, leaving a calm, clear pool into the depths of which you can peer.

EXERCISE 29

Stopping mental wandering

Koans are good to combine with meditation, to help in the mental clearance process. Here are versions of some that have been offered by various Zen Masters at various times. Work on one at a time for a few of your meditation sessions.

One moon reflects in every pool; every pool reflects the one moon.

What was my original face before my mother and father were born?

If I do not get it from myself, where will I go for it?

The entire sky is captured in one dewdrop on the grass.

On what does the centre point of the axle of a wheel turn?

Journey's end

Unfortunately, there is no direct way that a book can enable you to enter the Silence. Ironically, there is actually a classic work from 1920 entitled *How to Enter the Silence*, and although it provides some inspirational anecdotes and quotations its bottom line as to the 'how to' is, yes, meditation. The author, Helen Rhodes Wallace, promises, 'The guarantee of arrival is practice.'

For most of us, seeking spiritual insight through meditation will require a dedicated effort. But the journey becomes easier with time – practice makes perfect. Either mindfulness or single-point meditation (whether internally visualized or fixed on an external focus) are the most applicable types of meditation for seeking the Silence.

Not all of us will aspire to this deep, spiritual level of consciousness, and we may want to use meditation more modestly to counter daily stress, to help towards maintaining overall well-being, and for general personal insight and mental clarity. Hopefully, this book will provide you with sufficient knowledge about the nature and many forms of meditation for whatever level of use you choose to put it to. Remember what Sogyal Rinpoche told us earlier on in the book: 'The gift of learning to meditate is the greatest gift you can give yourself in this life. For it is only through meditation that you can undertake the journey to discover your true nature ... Meditation is the road to enlightenment.'

Appendix: Take Note

- Meditation, when correctly practised, is a maintained state of alert passivity, of sustained attention, and beginners need to be on guard against dozing off!

- Something to be aware of: when you have developed some proficiency in meditating, it can very occasionally happen that a powerful surge of energy is felt coursing up the spine. This is known in Hinduism by the Sanskrit word 'kundalini'.

In traditional beliefs, kundalini is considered to be a store of spiritual power made up of two energies known as ida and pingala. These energies reside at the base of the spine. However, under certain conditions, it is believed they are able to ascend a channel within the spinal cord. Ida and pingala rise up the spine separately – pingala on the right side and ida on the left – until they reach the sixth chakra (ajna) located between the eyebrows, at which point they cross over each other, providing the opportunity for breakthrough to the highest level, which is the seventh chakra (sahasrana). This final chakra is located at the top or crown of the head and is believed to be the doorway to cosmic consciousness or enlightenment.

If kundalini is awakened during deep meditation it is a real, physical sensation and can seem alarming and overwhelming if you are unprepared for it, but just let it happen, do not resist it. You are having a spiritual awakening and are indeed privileged. But afterwards, seek the counsel of an accomplished yoga teacher familiar with the esoteric aspects of yoga, so you can better handle another kundalini experience should one come along.

Resources

NOTE: Inclusion of organizations and online links in this brief selection does not necessarily mean I endorse them – I take no responsibility for them, and I have no financial connections with them. Rather, they are offered purely as information in order to help provide starting points for your own further enquiry.

CHAPTER TWO: MODERN MEDITATION
Association for Transpersonal Psychology
Official website: www.atpweb.org

The Theosophical Society, 50 Gloucester Place, Marylebone, London W1U 8EA (UK).
Webpage: http://theosophicalsociety.org.uk/about-us

Center for Mindfulness in Medicine, Healthcare, and Society (USA)
Website: https://www.umassmed.edu/cfm/mindfulness-based-programs/mbsr-courses/about-mbsr/history-of-mbsr/

Transcendental Meditation
Official website: https://www.tm.org/
UK website: http://uk.tm.org

Open Focus
UK website: www.openfocus.org.uk/
Other contact: https://openfocus.com/home/

CHAPTER THREE: MEDITATION, MEDICINE AND SCIENCE
National Center for Complementary and Integrative Health (USA)
Website: https://nccih.nih.gov

CHAPTER SIX: SINGLE-POINT MEDITATION
Drawing a mandala
https://www.craftsy.com/art/article/how-to-draw-a-mandala/

Buddhaghosa's The Path of Purification (Visuddhimagga) online
https://accesstoinsight.org/lib/authors/nanamoli/PathofPurification2011.pdf

YouTube item with powerful moving mandala imagery plus sound
https://www.youtube.com/watch?v=tpZsk7QqsMI

CHAPTER SEVEN: THE POWERS OF SOUND, LIGHT AND NATURE
YouTube colours of sound. Note: some items are preceded by brief adverts, but ignore them while setting up your session, or simply skip them.

White noise
https://www.youtube.com/watch?v=CCnCMHNyny8
(About one hour's duration.)

Pink noise
https://www.youtube.com/watch?annotation_id=annotation_979063657&feature=iv&src_vid=ZXtimhT-ff4&v=8SHf6wmX5MU
(About ten hours' duration. This site offers a dark screen option.)

Brown noise
https://www.youtube.com/watch?v=FcWgjCDPiP4
(Over one hour. As always if meditating, don't look at the video.)

YouTube nature sounds
Forest river
https://www.bing.com/videos/search?q=pure+natu
re+sounds&view=detail&mid=4532B4FDBAA3A
0D36FF64532B4FDBAA3A0D36FF6&FORM=V
IRE

Breaking surf
https://www.youtube.com/watch?v=31vyjO8N5hI&
t=0s&list=PL93A884519C98E32B&index=5

Waterfall
https://www.youtube.com/watch?v=IqKbOsMti7s

You can of course easily find sites online where
you can purchase CDs of natural sounds.

CHAPTER EIGHT: THE POWER OF SILENCE
YouTube sound of Tibetan singing bowls plus
running water https://www.youtube.com/
watch?v=RgqxZU6_qOY

YouTube OM mantra chant
https://www.youtube.com/watch?v=RIBJoCb6wys

Silence Tourism (just one example)
http://www.visitkarelia.fi/en/Travelling/Your-vacation/
Silence-Travel

Select Bibliography

INTRODUCTION

Harte, J.L., Eifert, G.H., and Smith, R., 1995. The effects of running and meditation on beta-endorphin, corticotropin-releasing hormone and cortisol in plasma, and on mood. *Biol. Psychol.* (NETHERLANDS), vol.40, no.3, June (pp.251–65).

Johns Hopkins Medicine, 2014. Meditation for anxiety, depression? *ScienceDaily*, 6 January.

Nidich, S.I., Rainforth, M.V., Haaga, D.A.F., et al., 2009. A randomized controlled trial on effects of the transcendental meditation program on blood pressure, psychological distress, and coping in young adults. *American Journal of Hypertension*, vol.22, no.12 (pp.1326–1331).

CHAPTER ONE: MEDITATION IN ANCIENT TRADITIONS

Devenish, R.P., 2013. *The Hermitage Meditation Manual*. San Francisco: Dharma Fellowship Publications.

Gibson, W., 1958. *The Key to Yoga*. East Brunswick: Bell Publishing Co.

Gilbert, R.A., 1991. *The Elements of Mysticism*. Rockport: Element Books.

Hardon, J.A., 1968. *Religions of the World*. New York: Image Books.

Herrigel, E., 1960. *The Method of Zen*. London: Arkana.

Khan, Pir Vilayat Inayat, 1974. *Towards the One*. New York: HarperCollins.

Laughlin, C.D., 2018. Neuroanthropology of meditation across cultures. *Time & Mind*, vol.11, no.3 (September). (In press at time of writing.)

Lings, M., 1995. *What is Sufism?* Santa Rosa: Atrium Publications.

Radhakrishnan, S., 1939/1969. *Eastern Religions and Western Thought*. New York: Oxford University Press.

Renou, L., 1962. *The Nature of Hinduism*. New York: Walker and Co.

Roland, P., 1999. *Kabbalah*. London: Piatkus.

Smith, H., 1958. *The Religions of Man*. New York: Harper & Row.

Sogyal Rinpoche, 1994. *Meditation*. San Francisco: Harper.

Watts, A.W., 1957. *The Way of Zen*. London: Thames & Hudson.

Worthington, V., 1989. *A History of Yoga*. London: Arkana.

CHAPTER TWO: MODERN MEDITATION

Barnes, P.M., Bloom, B., & Nahin, R., 2008. Complementary and alternative medicine use among adults and children: United States, 2007. *CDC National Health Statistics Report #12*.

Blavatsky, H.P., 1888. *The Secret Doctrine*. (Numerous current editions.)

Fehmi, L. and Robbins, J., 2007. *The Open-Focus Brain*. Boulder: Trumpeter.

Gotink, R.A., Meijboom, R., Vernooij, M.W., et al., 2016. 8-week Mindfulness Based Stress Reduction induces brain changes similar to traditional long-term meditation practice – a systematic review. *Brain and Cognition*, vol.108, October (pp.32–41).

James, W., 1902. *The Varieties of Religious Experiences*. London: Longmans, Green and Co.

Kabat-Zinn, J., 1994. *Wherever You Go, There You Are*. London: Piatkus.

Ram Dass, 1971. *Be Here Now*. San Cristobal: Lama Foundation.

Russell, P., 1978. *The TM Technique*. New York: Arkana.

CHAPTER THREE: MEDITATION, MEDICINE AND SCIENCE

Banquet, J.P., 1973. Spectral analysis of the EEG in meditation. *Electroencephalography and Clinical Neurophysiology*, 35, pp.143–151.

Benson, H., Bearly, J.F., Carol, M.P., 1974. The Relaxation Response. *Psychiatry*, Vol. 37.

Carrington, P., 1977. *Freedom in Meditation*. New York: Doubleday.

Cherkin, D.C., Sherman, K.J., Balderson, B.H., et al., 2016. Effect of mindfulness-based stress reduction vs cognitive behavioral therapy or usual care on back pain and functional limitations in adults with chronic low back pain: a randomized clinical trial. JAMA, 315 (12) (pp.1240–1249).

Cramer, H., Haller, H., Lauche, R., et al., 2012. Mindfulness-based stress reduction for low back pain. A systematic review. BMC Complementary and Alternative Medicine, 12(162):1–8.

Cramer, H., Lauche, R., Haller, H., et al., 2013. A systematic review and meta-analysis of yoga for low back pain. Clinical Journal of Pain, 29(5) (pp.450–60).

Dakwar, E. and Levin, F.R., 2009. The emerging role of meditation in addressing psychiatric illness, with a focus on substance use disorders. Harvard Review of Psychiatry, 17(4) (pp.254–267).

Desbordes, G., Negi, L.T., Pace, T.W. et al., 2012. Effects of mindful-attention and compassion meditation training on amygdala response to emotional stimula in an ordinary, non-meditative state. Frontiers in Human Neuroscience, 6:292.

Fehmi and Robbins, 2007, op. cit.

Gard, T., Hölzel, B.K., Lazar, S.W., 2014. The potential effects of meditation on age-related cognitive decline: a systematic review. Annals of the New York Academy of Sciences, 1307 (pp.89–103).

Garner, D., 2010. Tune In, Turn On, Turn Page. Book review, The New York Times, 8 January.

Glueck, B.C. and Stroebel, C.F., 1975. Biofeedback and meditation in the treatment of psychiatric illnesses. Comprehensive Psychiatry, Vol.16(4), pp.303–321.

Goldstein, C.M., Josephson, R., Xie, S., et al., 2012. Current perspectives on the use of meditation to reduce blood pressure. International Journal of Hypertension.

Goyal, M., Singh, S., Sibinga, E.M., et al., 2014. Meditation programs for psychological stress and well-being: a systematic review and meta-analysis. JAMA Internal Medicine, 174(3) (pp.357–368).

Hilton, L., Hempel, S., Ewing, B., et al., 2017. Mindfulness meditation for chronic pain: systematic review and meta-analysis. Ann. Behav. Med., 51(2) (pp.199–213).

Hines, T.M., 1998. Comprehensive review of biorhythm theory. Psychological Reports; Sage Journals, August.

Kabat-Zinn, J. and Davidson, R.J., 2011. The Mind's Own Physician: a Scientific Dialogue with the Dalai Lama on the Healing Power of Meditation. Oakland: New Harbinger Publications.

Kok, B.E., Singer, T., 2017. Phenomenological fingerprints of four meditations: differential state changes in affect, mind-wandering, meta-cognition, and interoception before and after daily practice across 9 months of training. Mindfulness, 8(1).

Laughlin, C.D., 2018. op cit.

Lopes, J., Arnosti, D., et al., 2016. Melatonin decreases estrogen receptor binding to estrogen response elements sites on the OCT4 gene in human breast cancer stem cells. Genes and Cancer, 107.

Luders, E., 2013. Exploring age-related brain degeneration in meditation practitioners. Annals of the New York Academy of Sciences, 1307 (pp.82–88).

Luders, E., Kurth, F., Mayer, E.A., et al., 2012. The unique brain anatomy of meditation practitioners: alterations in cortical gyrification. Frontiers in Human Neuroscience, 6:1–9.

Massion, A.O., Teas, J., Herbert, J.R., Wertheimer, M.D., Kabat-Zinn, J., 1995. Meditation, melatonin and breast/prostate cancer: hypothesis and preliminary data. Medical Hypotheses, 44:1, pp.39–46.

Maxfield, M.C., 1990. Effects of rhythmic drumming on EEG and subjective experience. Unpublished dissertation. Institute of Transpersonal Psychology.

Moltz, D., 1976. Effects of internally generated sounds on mood. Senior thesis, Princeton University.

Neher, A., 1961. Auditory driving observed with scalp electrodes in normal subjects. Electroenceph. Clin. Neurophysiol. 13 (pp.449–451).

Neher, A., 1962. A physiological explanation of unusual behavior in ceremonies involving drums. Human Biology, IV (pp.151–160).

Ong, J.C., Manber, R., Segal, Z., et al., 2014. A randomized controlled trial of mindfulness meditation for chronic insomnia. Sleep, 37(9) (pp.1553–1563).

Orme-Johnson, D.W., 1973. Autonomic stability and transcendental meditation. *Psychosomatic Medicine*, 35 (4), (pp.341–349).

Reiner, K., Tibi, L., Lipsitz, J.D., 2013, Do mindfulness-based interventions reduce pain intensity? A critical review of the literature. *Pain Med.*, 14(2), pp.230–242.

Robinson, R.H., 1970. The Three Trainings. *Man, Myth and Magic*, vol.3, Marshall Cavendish Corporation (p.355).

Rosenkranz, M.A., et al., 2013. A comparison of mindfulness-based stress reduction and an active control in modulation of neurogenic inflammation. *Brain Behav Immun.*, 27C (pp.174–184).

Singh, R. 1998. *Self-healing: Powerful Techniques*. California: SRF Publishers.

Wallace, R.K., 1971. *The Physiological Effects of Transcendental Meditation: A Proposed Fourth Major State of Consciousness*. Students' International Meditation Society, 2nd ed.

Wong, C., 2018. The connection between melatonin and meditation. Very Well Mind. Available at: https://www.verywellmind.com/melatonin-and-meditation-88370

CHAPTER FOUR: THE BASICS OF PRACTICAL MEDITATION

Brennan, R., 2017. *How to Breathe*. London: Eddison Books Ltd.

Devereux, C., 1993. *The Aromatherapy Kit*. London: Headline Book Publishing.

Devereux, C., and Stockel, F., 1997. *The Meditation Kit*. Boston: Journey Editions.

Gibson, W., 1958, op. cit.

Swami Rama, Ballentine, R. and Hymes, A., 1979. *Science of Breath*. Honesdale, Pennsylvania: Himalayan International Institute.

Tucci, G., 1973. *The Theory and Practice of the Mandala*. York Beach, Maine: Samuel Weiser.

Wallace, H., 1920. *How to Enter the Silence*. Massachusetts: The Elizabeth Towne Co., Inc

CHAPTER FIVE: GUIDED VISUALIZATION: STARTING THE INNER JOURNEY

Jung, C.G., 1956. *Symbols of Transformation*. Princeton: Bollington Series (1967 edition).

Jung, C.G., 1959/1968. *The Archetypes and the Collective Unconscious* (Collected Works of C.G. Jung). London: Routledge.

Roland, P., 1999, op. cit.

CHAPTER SIX: SINGLE-POINT MEDITATION

Buddhaghosa, B. (trans. by Bhikkhu Nanamoli), 1975/1991/1999. *The Path of Purification*. Onalaska: BPS Pariyatti Editions. (The original *Visuddhimagga* was written in the fifth century. Various recent and current editions exist.)

Jung, C.G., 1961. *Memories, Dreams, Reflections*. London: Fontana, 1995. (There are various current editions.)

Jung, C.G., 1969. *Mandala Symbolism*. Princeton: Princeton University Press.

Laughlin, C.D., McManus, J. and d'Aquili, E.G., 1990. *Brain, Symbol and Experience*. New York: Columbia University Press (1992 edn.).

Malville, J. McKim, 1993. Astronomy at Vijayanagara: Sacred Geography Confronts the Cosmos. *In*: Rana P.B. Singh (eds.) *The Spirit and Power of Place*. Benares Hindu University: National Geographic Society of India.

CHAPTER SEVEN: THE POWERS OF SOUND, LIGHT AND NATURE

Dewdney, S. and Kidd, K.E., 1962. *Indian Rock Paintings of the Great Lakes*. Toronto: University of Toronto Press.

Dowson, T.A., 1992. *Rock Engravings of Southern Africa*. Johannesburg: Witwatersrand University Press.

Hesse, H., 1922. *Siddhartha*. London: Picador (1991 edn.).

Jaynes, J., 1976. *The Origin of Consciousness in the Breakdown of the Bicameral Mind*. Boston: Houghton Mifflin.

Laughlin, C.D., 2018, op. cit.

Levin, T. and Suzukei, V., 2006. *Where Rivers and Mountains Sing: Sound, Music and Nomadism in Tuva and Beyond*. Bloomington: Indiana University Press.

Lewis-Williams, D. and Dowson, T., 1989. *Images of Power*. Johannesburg: Southern Book Publishers.

Rajnovich, G., 1994. *Reading Rock Art: Interpreting the Indian Rock Paintings of the Canadian Shield*. Toronto: Natural Heritage/Natural History Inc.

Whitley, D.S., 1996. *A Guide to Rock Art Sites*. Missoula: Mountain Press.

CHAPTER EIGHT: THE POWER OF SILENCE

Aldridge, D. and Fachner, J. (eds.), 2006. *Music and Altered States*. London: Jessica Kingsley, p.167.

Bernardi, L., Porta, C. and Sleight, P., 2006. Cardiovascular, cerebrovascular, and respiratory changes induced by different types of music in musicians and non-musicians: the importance of silence. *Heart*, vol.92, no.4 (pp.445–452).

Kirste, I., Nicola, Z., Kronenberg, G., Walker, T.L., Liu, R.C. and Kempermann, G., 2015. Is silence golden? Effects of auditory stimuli and their absence on adult hippocampal neurogenesis.

Brain Structure and Function, vol.220, no.2 (pp.1221–1228).

Komppula, R., Raija, K.H. and Vikman, N., 2017. Listening to the sounds of silence: Forest Based Wellbeing Tourism in Finland. In: Joseph S. Chen and Nina K. Prebensen (eds.) *Nature Tourism*. London: Routledge (pp. 120–130).

Laughlin, C.D., 2011. *Communing with the Gods*. Brisbane: Daily Grail Publishing.

Moran, J.M., Kelley, W.M. and Heatherton, T.F., 2013. What can the organization of the brain's default mode network tell us about self-knowledge? *Frontiers in Human Neuroscience*, vol.7.

Nemeth, E., Pieretti, N., Zollinger, S.A., et al., 2013. Bird song and anthropogenic noise: vocal constraints may explain why birds sing higher-frequency songs in cities. *Proceedings of the Royal Society B*.

Sogyal Rinpoche, 1994. *Meditation*. London: Rider (p.5).

Wallace, Helen Rhodes, 1920. *How to Enter the Silence*. (Kessinger edn.)

Waugh, R., 2012. Bird song has got LOUDER in the last 30 years to compete with traffic – and the tunes are changing too. London: *Daily Mail*, 3 April.

Index

Acknowledgements

My first introduction to meditation was in 1977, when I met my late 'spiritual mother', Fran Stockel, and joined a weekly meditation group that she hosted. And when I wrote *The Meditation Kit* in 1997, she was present to contribute her thoughts about the four meditation themes that were a major part of that book. Among others who have inspired me at various times on what I might grandly call my spiritual journey include: Shirley Cohen, Eva and Eugene Graf, Marcy Losapio, Maria McKenna, Dorothy Odle, Deepa Patel, and Mary Jane Ridder. And participation in the guided meditations of the Sufi teachers, the late Pir Inyat Khan and his son, Pir Zia, brought my experience of meditation to a whole new level.

For help with this present book, which aims to bring in some unfamiliar approaches to the practice of meditation, I am indebted to neuroanthropologist Charles Laughlin for so generously letting me access to his amazing paper on *Neuroanthropology of Meditation Across Cultures* prior to its publication. It proved most helpful for the first chapter on Ancient Traditions, and, indeed, his other writings and experience of Dream Yoga meditation with Tibetan teachers have also proved insightful. I am equally grateful to my husband, Paul, for providing me with information on various aspects of sound, along with ideas for some visualization themes — and for always being there for me.

Finally, special thanks go to Lisa Dyer and, especially Tessa Monina, for their support throughout the writing of the book; Jane Struthers for her editing skills, Nanette Hoogslag for the beautiful illustrations that bring so much to the work, and to Nick Eddison who made this book possible in the first place.

Picture credits:
Wikimedia Commons 98 Kosi Gramatikoff; 100 Baldiri;
101 Gunawan Kartapranta; 105 N. Manytchkine

Eddison Books Limited
Managing Director Lisa Dyer
Managing Editor Tessa Monina
Copy Editor Jane Struthers
Proofreader Jane Donovan
Indexer Angie Hipkin
Designer Brazzle Atkins
Production Sarah Rooney

Illustrations by Nanette Hoogslag